♦ 100 ♦ BEST BALTI CURRIES

DIANE LOWE was born in Worcestershire and spent her formative curry-eating years in the Midlands where she trained as a graphic designer at Birmingham College of Art.
She moved to London to pursue a career as an advertising copywriter, and during the past three years has spent most of her spare time in the Baltihouses of Birmingham, watching the chefs at work, uncovering the secrets of Balti cooking and recreating the recipes in her own kitchen.

MIKE DAVIDSON is an illustrator and lecturer in graphic design, living in Henley-on-Thames. He has had a lifetime love of Asian food, which got off to a shaky start when he picked out the sultanas from a very unauthentic school-dinner curry! He has travelled all over India, sampling food from places as diverse as the Lake Palace Hotel in Udaipur to the street vendors of Delhi, purposely choosing items on the menu he had never tried before. The discovery of a whole new cuisine in 'Balti' was a revelation, and visiting the Baltihouses in the Midlands researching this book, a delight.

◆ 100 ◆
BEST
BALTI
CURRIES

Authentic Dishes

from the Baltihouses

◆

DIANE LOWE

MIKE DAVIDSON

PAVILION

To Adam, Fan and Alice

First published in Great Britain in 1994 by
Pavilion Books Limited
26 Upper Ground, London SE1 9PD

Designed by Elizabeth Ayer

A CIP catalogue record for this book is available from the British Library

ISBN 1 85793 221 8

Printed and bound in Great Britain by Butler and Tanner Ltd,
Frome and London

10 9 8 7 6 5 4 3

This book may be ordered by post direct from the publisher.
Please contact the Marketing Department. But try your bookshop first.

CONTENTS

INTRODUCTION

After partition took place in India in 1947, creating Muslim Pakistan, many Muslims left to build new lives in cities far removed from their own culture and climate. Many came to Birmingham to work and were allocated housing in one of the poorest neighbourhoods in the city, often in near-condemned properties no-one else wanted to live in. Over the years the community grew and thrived, carving out a 2 square mile radius for itself and transforming it into 'Little Pakistan'.

During the austere post-war years the piercingly bright, clashing colours of saris began to illuminate the streets of Birmingham, and shops that had once been Victorian poulterers, haberdashers and cheesemongers became outlets for a whole range of goods imported from Pakistan. Weird and wonderful vegetables were stacked on trestle tables outside greengrocers; mounds of spices – from the yellow ochre of turmeric to the terracotta of paprika – were sold loose over counters. Rustic looking cooking implements swung from nails outside shop fronts that still had their bow windows, original doors and shop fittings intact. Sign writers gradually replaced the faded names of 19th century family businesses with the extravagant dots and curves of Islamic characters. The effect of all this bustling Asian influence cut a colourful swathe through Birmingham's drab industrial landscape and still does.

The Pakistanis who settled in Birmingham tended to originate from the north of the region, so restaurants (very few in number until the 70s) were modelled on the small, simple establishments of Northern Pakistan which are rather like our transport cafés. For years they catered solely for Asians. At the same time elsewhere in the city, Indian restaurants were making their debut. Their menus were sparse: meat or chicken curries in three strengths - hot, very hot and mind-numbingly hot. These were eaten with a basic vegetable dish and boiled rice and enjoyed with hearty enthusiasm by non-Asians.

In the main these curries weren't prepared with the traditional subtle blend of spices as in India but with chilli powder applied with a spade, in the belief that that's what the Brummie customers wanted. And for a very long time they did. Hot, Madras and Vindaloo, with a milder version for women, reigned supreme for a decade, with more and more restaurants springing up to meet demand. The student population in particular seemed to have an unlimited appetite for this exotic, reasonably priced food and they frequented curry houses in their droves. Amongst the Brummie male population, seeing who could down the hottest curry became a popular post-closing-time pastime. Even with the popularity of spicy food, few non-Asians ate in Little Pakistan.

It wasn't until the early 70s that one place caught the attention of those seeking something different. Here the chef cooked and served his curry in a small wok. The meal was known as a Balti. Instead of having a paint-stripping effect on the roof of your mouth, each individual ingredient sang through and an entirely new taste, unfamiliar to curry enthusiasts, was born.

The basis of virtually every Balti is a blend of onion, tomato and fresh coriander. From this starting point anything can happen, and it does. Today there are around 80 Baltihouses in and around the city. Most are in what used to be Little Pakistan, now known proudly as the Balti Belt.

What is a Balti?

Balti is the name both of the metal bowl shaped like a wok (this is also sometimes called a karahi) and, confusingly, the meal or dish cooked in it.

That Northern Pakistan's proximity to China resulted in the cross-fertilisation of cultures, with the wok finding its way across the border, is undoubtedly true because Balti is 'a curry cooked in a wok'. The word 'balti' actually means bucket. But none of this helps to uncover Balti's roots. We take the view of a number of restaurants that Balti is a truly Brummie phenomenon which goes back as far as 1975! The fiercest debate you'll hear in the Midlands is not of Balti's ancient origins but who opened the very first Baltihouse and so set the ball rolling.

Balti uses fresh meat, vegetables and its own distinctive range of spices, with the focus on fresh coriander and methi (fenugreek). There's a sauce, or 'gravy' as it is unromantically known, made up mainly of onions and tomatoes, and a gently aromatic marinade for the meat. It's eaten not with cutlery or with rice but with bread (naan or chapati). You simply break a piece off, spoon up the mixture with it (use your right hand only to be correct) and pop it into your mouth. The beauty of Balti is that with relatively little time and effort you can produce a stir-fried dish that tastes utterly authentic to the region (Birmingham, if not Pakistan). The time is taken up making the Balti sauce and marinading the meat, and even that doesn't take long.

Over the years we have eaten hundreds of Baltihouse Baltis. No two are ever the same. Until we became curious as to why, got to know the chefs and were let in on their secrets, none of these recipes was ever written down or shared with anyone outside the chef's immediate family.

The Balti Belt

Birmingham has always been known as the second city. For many non-Brummies that meant second-best, a poor number two to London – a city in the heart of England without a clearly defined identity. But today Birmingham is very much on Britain's culinary map, since the Baltihouse phenomenon has mushroomed into cult status. In less than 20 years, an area of around 5 km / 3 miles square has spawned no less than 56 Baltihouses. The area is tagged the Balti Belt.

The suburbs have also caught on and another 30 or so restaurants have sprouted up and enjoy a roaring trade. Even Stratford-upon-Avon has its Baltihouses. So does genteel Leamington Spa. Barmouth in Wales and Southampton have both acquired them and, at the time of writing, London too has jumped on the bandwagon, with a number of authentic Baltihouses. Balti bingeing looks set to become a favourite pastime for us all, rather than the privileged few.

The man who has done most to spread the word in the Midlands on the Baltihouse Experience is Andy Munro. He is the author of the specialist restaurant guide 'The Essential Street Balti Guide' which is now in its third reprint. For Balti Freaks this is The Bible. Andy is acknowledged as the expert on the development of the Balti scene in Birmingham. He says, 'My Restaurant Guide is deliberately off-the-wall in style to reflect my belief that Balti cooking is a sort of Asian fun food. You can mix and match ingredients almost pizza-fashion, to create your own particular Balti. My enthusiasm for the experience is total following my conversion nearly 10 years ago in a restaurant in the Handsworth area. My Balti could have been an even hotter experience the next week as that same Baltihouse was burnt

down in the Handsworth disturbances! I rarely bother with an ordinary curry these days because I believe Balti is Asian cooking "live".'

The Baltihouse

Whereas the Balti is a sophisticated eating experience, the places in which it's eaten are not. Baltihouses have a unique style - they have developed a look and atmosphere all their own, based on the original transport café type eating houses of Pakistan. Seating is usually basic, tables have menus under glass tops. Starters and sweets are displayed in cold cabinets as there is always a brisk take-away trade. Service in the main restaurant is conducted at lightning speed as there's usually a long queue at the door.

Balti-holics who come to eat cover a wide age-span. Children are welcome, as most premises are unlicensed, being Muslim owned. Diners bring their own drinks, usually bought from the 'offie' (off licence) round the corner, which in some cases is owned by a relative of the proprietor.

THE BALTI KITCHEN

EQUIPMENT

The utensils you'll need to make success-ful Baltis are few. You'll probably find you have most of them in your kitchen already.

The first thing you'll need is a wok – or preferably two if you want to cook a meat dish and a vegetable accompaniment at the same time. Alternatively you can use a large frying pan. When the food is cooked, simply serve it in individual bowls. Or, for those of you who want your Baltis utterly authentic, you'll prefer to cook and serve in the 'karahi' or Balti dish, as they do in Birmingham.

This is a rounded pan, like a wok, with one or two ring handles. It became the all-purpose cooking pan in Northern Pakistan thousands of years ago and has changed little since. It comes in several sizes: the largest is a whopping 92 cm / 3 feet in diameter and the smallest is a minute 8 cm / 3 1/4 inches.

In Baltihouses individual Baltis are cooked and served in small karahis, usually 18 cm / 7 inch ones. Since the old days the base of the karahi has been flattened out a bit to accommodate the modern stove, and today the dishes are made from pressed steel as well as cast iron. They are available at almost every hardware shop in the Balti Belt, and from our own special mail order house (page 157). You'll need two wok-size Balti dishes and as many 18 cm / 7 in ones as you're expecting guests.

CLEANING YOUR BALTI DISH

If you use a wok regularly you may have a bamboo bristle wok-cleaning brush. This is perfect for cleaning most authentic Balti dishes too. Dishwashing machines are firmly out for these pans. However, there are black-enamelled, white-speckled Balti dishes and stainless steel ones available that are very easy to care for and dish-washer-proof.

BALTI DISH ACCESSORIES

You will need very few and these are borrowed mainly from the wok. At the same hardware stores you can buy wooden stands to rest your karahis on when you take them off the stove. You can also buy stainless steel stands. You will sometimes need lids, and a wok spatula also comes in handy.

Other equipment

chopping board
good sharp knives
mezzaluna (a semicircular-bladed chop-ping utensil)
a ladle (7 tablespoons capacity)
mortar and pestle
metal sieve
saucepan for deep frying
long-handled strainer for removing deep-fried food
large metal spoon for stir-frying
large slotted metal spoon
wooden spoon
range of saucepans with lids

oven tray

grill tray with wire rack

large saucepan with lid for making gravy

non-metallic dish for marinading meat

cast-iron tava (from specialist shops or our
own mail-order house, page 157)

Gadgets

THE BLENDER

Nothing beats an ordinary blender for
purées as anyone who has introduced a
baby to solids will know. It is invaluable
in several Balti processes - especially Balti
sauce and Balti dip preparation.

THE FOOD PROCESSOR

Chops, mixes and blends most ingredients
and with its added attachments is useful
for vegetable slicing and shredding,
mixing dough and grinding spices.

THE COFFEE GRINDER

In our experience this is the best machine
for grinding spices. Gently roast the spices
first. We use a 10-year-old Moulinex that,
despite its age, grinds beautifully to any
fineness you want.

THE FREEZER

As we have already said, Balti uses mainly
fresh ingredients. When you are catering
for many on a regular basis, little is wasted.
But at home, the freezer means you can pre-
cook some parts of the process or preserve
ingredients that are not available on a
daily basis (certain herbs, for example)

or freeze quantities of Balti sauce. The
sauce, as we shall see, is the basis of
almost all Balti dishes. In our recipes we
make enough for 4 servings at least. You
might double or quadruple the quantities
and freeze the extra, so that you are
prepared for your next Balti. Also, any
tandoori marinade that remains after
removing the meat to be cooked, can be
frozen and used once more.

The freezer is obviously ideal for
storing cooked Baltis. When you do this,
remember to undercook by about 5 minutes
to allow for catching-up in reheating.
Remove any whole spices before freezing
as they tend to deteriorate. Seal in an air-
tight container because spicy food can
affect everything else in the compartment.
Adjust the spices and seasoning after
reheating.

THE MICROWAVE

This is perfect for defrosting and reheating
Baltis, but don't use it for reheating anything that has been deep fried. The crisp
outer coating will emerge soggy from the
microwave.

BALTI INGREDIENTS

Meat Baltis should have bite-size pieces
of meat in a sauce of a thickish creamy
consistency. Vegetables should also be
prepared in chunk-size pieces. In Pakistan,
Karahi dishes are much drier than their
Birmingham equivalents. If you prefer
them dry you simply add less Balti sauce.

All the ingredients you need to make most of the recipes in this book are available in supermarkets, though a wider range of fresh chillies, spices and unusual vegetables are to be found on fresh-produce stalls in areas that have Asian, Greek, Turkish or West Indian communities, at prices that are keener than any super-market can offer.

Here is a list of all the ingredients you will be using in this book:

Fresh ingredients

apples
aubergines
basil
broccoli
cauliflowers
chillies – fresh green, fat or long and thin
    fresh red, small fiery ones
coriander
courgettes
cream – single and double
garlic
ginger
grapes
green peppers
ladies fingers (bhindi or okra)
lemons
limes
methi (fenugreek)
mushrooms
onions
parsley
peas
potatoes

olive oil
pears
spinach
vegetable oil
yoghurt, plain

Dry ingredients

baking powder
bay leaves
beans, dried – red kidney and black eye
cardamom pods – brown and green
cardamom, ground
cayenne pepper
chick peas, dried
chilli powder
chillies – dried red, whole and crushed
cinnamon sticks
cloves
coconut, desiccated
coconut cream
coriander seeds, ground
cumin seeds – black and green
cumin seeds, ground
curry powder – shop bought
fennel seeds
flour – plain, wholemeal chapatti and gram
food colourings – orange, red and yellow
lentils – green, orange and yellow
paprika
peas, dried split
peppercorns, black
salt
sesame seeds
star anise
stock cubes – chicken bouillon and
    vegetable

turmeric powder
vanilla pods
yeast

Specialist ingredients

A few of the recipes call for these. Purists will probably want to hunt them down and put them to use. Everything listed below is available from Asian suppliers. In most cases the ingredient is optional or we suggest a substitute, so don't worry if it's not available where you live.

amchur (dried mango powder)
ajwan (lovage seeds)
char mugaz (dried melon seeds)
galangal, dried and fresh (related to ginger
   which can be used instead)
ghee, butter or vegetable
gram flour (made from milling chick peas
and often used in batters)
kaffir lime leaves
karela, tinda, lotus root (exotic vegetables
   sold fresh and canned)
kalonji (onion seeds)
kewra essence (plant extract used in
   flavouring desserts)
mustard leaf
tamarind – block or jar of extract
tandoori masala – paste or powder

Ingredients for sweets

caster sugar
evaporated milk
ground rice flour
green cardamoms
ground almonds
cashew nuts
milk, fresh
pistachio nuts, unsalted
rosewater
vermicelli

OIL AND GHEE

Oil is a very important ingredient in the making of a Balti. Most recipes use vegetable oil or a good quality corn or sunflower oil. Indian cooking never uses olive oil but a couple of Balti chefs do.

In a number of recipes we've used a clarified butter called ghee which is widely used in Pakistan and the Kashmiri regions. It's available all over the country in most supermarkets now and through Asian suppliers. There are two varieties – butter ghee and vegetable ghee. It is especially good in naan breads as it imparts a distinctive flavour to the dough. However, if you can't get ghee or don't want to use it because of its high cholesterol content you can substitute vegetable oil.

HERBS

Fresh coriander features prominently in Balti dishes. It looks like flat-leaf parsley but has a very distinctive taste. It is found in shops and market stalls in areas where there is an ethnic population (West Indian as well as Asian) and prepacked in small quantities in supermarkets. When you find it cheap, you can chop the leaves, discarding the bigger stalks, and freeze them in ice-cube trays. Fresh coriander can also be bought in pots, so you can keep it growing on your windowsill. And you can buy it dried in glass jars in the spice section of most supermarkets.

Methi (fenugreek) is also used in most of the recipes. Like coriander it is readily available fresh in areas with a high ethnic population, but almost never elsewhere. However, dried methi is very convenient, and is used by many if not most of the Baltihouses. Fresh methi can easily be grown on the windowsill and also frozen in the same way as coriander. It is one of the seeds popular in primary schools to show children the growing cycle, because it is very fast to sprout.

SPICES

Commercially ground spices are available everywhere in shops and supermarkets. They are ground in the factory and their storage life is about three months. Ideally spices would be ground each time you needed them, but this is obviously not practical. The best compromise is to grind whole spices yourself and to store them carefully.

Grinding your own spice is very simple and the result will be fresher than store-bought ground spice. Store your freshly ground spices in glass coffee jars, out of direct sunlight, in a cool, dry place. Dark glass is best because sunlight will affect the taste of the spice after a while. It is, of course, a shame to have to hide such wonderfully exotic colours and shapes in a cupboard. It's up to you! Remember to label each jar.

Grinding spices

There are a couple of spices that are too fibrous for home grinding and those are turmeric and ginger. Commercially ground ones are fine. Black and white pepper and paprika should also be bought ground. Use these in recipes that require specific amounts, e.g. $1/2$ teaspoon. In the final stages of cooking adjust seasoning if necessary with the pepper mill. A number of spices, in particular the oilier ones, are easier to grind if you roast them first.

As we said before, the best utensil for grinding spices is a coffee grinder. You could also use a mortar and pestle, although this obviously will take more effort.

Roasting spices

Brown cardamoms, cumin, coriander, methi seeds, bay leaves and cloves are ideally suited to the roasting process and the aroma that will pervade your kitchen will get your gastric juices going in preparation for your first home-cooked Balti. The word 'roasting' is a slight misnomer, because you can either use a frying pan on top of the oven (no oil in the pan), the grill or the oven. Each spice merely has to be heated long enough to release its aroma. A medium heat rather than hot is enough to do this.

For oven roasting, preheat the oven to 160°C / 325°F / gas mark 3 and allow no more than 10 minutes. Don't let the spices burn or blacken. A lightly roasted brown is the effect to aim for. Frying-pan roasting is the best method for beginners because you can see what you're doing from start to finish.

Blending spices or spice masala

Many Balti recipes call for garam masala. 'Garam' means hot, 'masala', mixed. Every Baltihouse uses a different masala. Most grind and mix their own cocktail of spices, but each is the unique combination that makes Balti cooking so distinctive from ordinary curries. On pages 25-26 we include three simple garam masala recipes. However, Waitrose, Tesco, Sainsbury and Safeway do sell reasonably good garam masalas if you prefer to use a commercial mixture. A particularly good home roasted and ground garam masala is available through our own mail order company (see page 157 for details).

MEAT

Lamb or mutton and chicken are the meats used to make every restaurant's Baltis. It's astonishing that with the use of just three types of meat, such a variety of different tasting dishes can be achieved. Offal from the sheep also features in a few of our Balti recipes. The diet in Northern Pakistan was mainly vegetarian though meat features nowadays more and more.

Halal meat

Balti is a Muslim cuisine. In this faith, there are strict rules on diet, which are called Halal (the Muslim equivalent of the Jewish Kosher). Besides the restrictions on alcohol, Halal forbids the consumption of pork but not of shellfish.

Muslims must shop at Halal butchers. Halal prescribes the killing, bleeding, cleaning and hanging of meat according to the principles of the Muslim religion. The lamb we buy in butchers or supermarkets tends to be fattier than Halal lamb so using the best and leanest cuts is important.

Lamb and mutton

Balti dishes almost always use meat off-the-bone. If you are par-cooking the meat you can use cuts on or off the bone - the former will impart a tastier flavour to the meat.

Leg of lamb is excellent. Even better, but more expensive, is lean and tender leg steak. When in season, half shoulders, knuckle end of English lamb, although fattier than leg, give a subtle, sweet taste to a dish. Cubed meat from the leg (as sold for kebabs) is available in butchers and supermarkets. Mutton (from sheep as opposed to lamb) is still sold by butchers but less and less often. It takes longer to cook to tenderness than lamb and you must remove as much fat as you can before cooking. Many of our recipes use minced lamb which again is widely available, fresh or frozen.

For any of the lamb, minced lamb or mutton recipes in the book you could substitute beef if you prefer.

Poultry and game

Chicken joints are widely used in Balti cooking. Quail is the only feathered game traditionally used – a rare link with Balti's origins in Pakistan where it is a common meat. Quail is not used so widely nowadays in Birmingham. We give recipes for quail as starter and as main course, both delicious.

CHICKEN

Chicken removed from the bone and diced (as much as you can dice such untidy meat!) is used for almost all chicken Baltis. Easiest to prepare is boned breast, but it's also the most expensive cut. Using breast on-the-bone will save a little money (removing the meat is easier after pre-cooking if there is any), or you can use a whole chicken, slicing meat from the bone in its uncooked state (a bit fiddly) or removing the meat after pre-cooking which is much easier. Skin must always be removed and discarded before cooking.

FEATHERED AND FURRED GAME

Karahi quail has long been a favourite in Northern Pakistan. It makes a rich, savoury Balti that is quick and easy to rustle up. In Britain, quail is bred specifically for eating, so you'll generally find it fresh in the larger supermarket chains and at good butchers. In the run-up to Christmas the supply is obviously more plentiful. The same goes for venison which nowadays is found all the year round. It too is now bred for the table. Venison Balti is a real treat.

Offal

Sheep's liver and kidney and even chicken livers are all used to make Balti meals. They lend themselves well to the stir-frying process. Brain Balti is served in Pakistan but this particular offal is hard to find and isn't everyone's cup of tea.

Fish and shellfish

Baltihouses are quite quirky in their choice of fish - some might even say downright eccentric ! You'll find everything from fresh fish to canned fish, even oysters.

Silver hake is just about the only fresh fish used, because in Baltis it's the tastiest and has the least bones. In fishmongers it is available as steaks, tails (on-the-bone) or fillets. It is served as a starter (fish tikka or fish tandoori) and used in a range of delicious main-course Baltis.

Prawns are widely used, from the large king or tiger prawns to the smallest that are found fresh or frozen in supermarkets. Because of the mix-and-match nature of Balti you'll often find prawn with lamb, prawn with minced meat (keema), as well as chicken and prawn Baltis. Canned sardines even put in a brief appearance! We've included a delicious Balti oyster recipe that is served in only one restaurant, and our own recipe for Balti mussels. And there's a terrific lobster Balti when you really want to push the boat out.

VEGETABLES AND VEGETARIAN BALTIS

We always say that if, as carnivores, we ever became vegetarians, Balti would make the change painless. Vegetable Baltis are numerous, deliciously different and, due to the rapid stir-frying process, sometimes preceded only by microwaving or steaming, highly nutritious. A Balti transforms even the blandest vegetable into a gently aromatic arena for the taste buds.

In ancient civilizations, spices, herbs and vegetables traditionally enjoyed a dual role – medicinal as well as culinary. Most of the spices used in Balti are also used, for instance, to treat cuts (turmeric), aid digestion (fennel seeds), reduce cholesterol (raw garlic), ease the symptoms of flu (methi), or even cure you of wind, as fresh ginger is said to do! (Melon seeds are said to help a late developing child to talk.) Fresh vegetables provide us with much-needed fibre as well as vitamins and minerals.

We've listed most of the vegetables used in Baltihouses. When you've become a dab hand you can improvise and add any vegetable that takes your fancy.

BASIC BALTI PREPARATION

In Northern Pakistan you would choose your Karahi ingredients from the meat and fresh produce on display in the restaurant, then you'd wash your hands, run what errands you have and afterwards take your seat. It would take 45 minutes in all while your meal cooked slowly in the wok – three-quarters of an hour because everything, including the meat is cooked from its raw state. Conversely one of the many attractions of the Midlands' Baltihouses is the speed with which your Balti arrives sizzling at your table.

Balti as 'fast food' has become part of the culinary tradition in Birmingham. To achieve this, but still retain the delicious balance of spicy flavours that infuse the ingredients to their very core, the chefs marinade, par-cook meat and vegetables in selected spices, and pay great attention to the taste and consistency of their pre-prepared Balti sauce. The final stage – the bringing together of all the elements in the Balti dish – is over in minutes, because all the work has been done beforehand. Here we show you exactly how the Baltihouses do it.

Baltis come in 5-stage, 4-stage, 3-stage, 2-stage and even 1-stage versions.

In the 5-stage method you'll be:
1. Marinading the meat
2. Par-cooking it

3. Making the Balti sauce
4. Making a special purée or sauce
5. Stir-frying it all together with extra ingredients and spices in the wok.

In the 4-stage method you'll be:
1. Marinading the meat
2. Par-cooking it
3. Making the Balti sauce
4. Stir-frying it all together with extra ingredients and spices in the wok.

In the 3-stage method you'll be:
1. Par-cooking the meat or fish in spices
2. Making the Balti sauce
3. Stir-frying it all together with extra ingredients and spices in the wok.

In the 2-stage method you'll be:
1. Making the Balti sauce
2. Stir-frying raw meat with the sauce and extra ingredients and spices in the wok.

In the 1-stage method you'll be:
1. Stir-frying meat, other ingredients and spices in the wok without adding Balti sauce.

BALTI AT A GLANCE

In this book we include only a few 5- and 4-stage recipes. Obviously 3- and 4-stage cooking takes a little more time, but it doesn't necessarily mean these recipes are more complicated. At the beginning of each recipe we tell you how many stages there are. We label each recipe as suitable for a quick meal, for instance, mild enough for children, ideal for all the family, perfect for a dinner party or a very special occasion. This way you can pick your Balti at a glance to fit in with the time you want to spend cooking or the occasion you're cooking for.

Balti sauce

Each chef has his own recipe for Balti sauce. And his, of course, is always the best, the one that gives his Baltis the edge! In truth they're all delicious and they're all different. Balti sauce is liquidised onion, tomato, water or stock and spices. It's the different blend of spices that makes each Baltihouse sauce different. In addition to giving a couple of restaurants' 'secret' sauces, we include one of our own you can make up and use in all the main course Baltis in the book if you prefer. We also show how you can subtly alter the taste of any of the sauces, by adding a bouquet garni of extra spices.

Balti marinading

Raw chicken, lamb, beef and fish for starters and main courses are often marinaded in spices beforehand. Make up the required mixture, mix with the meat and place in a shallow non-metallic dish with a sheet of foil or cling film as a lid. Marinade overnight if possible, although 2-3 hours will do at a pinch.

Balti par-cooking

Meat is often par-cooked with a bouquet of spices prior to stir-frying in the Balti dish. This infuses the meat with the spice flavour. With mutton it also tenderises the meat. Par-cooking is particularly good for fattier cuts of meat because you can skim the fat from the surface before using the meat for Balti-ing.

Balti stir-frying

This last stage is done quickly, so have all your final ingredients finely chopped, ground or puréed to hand. Lay everything you need out in little bowls. Add each ingredient in rapid succession to your wok and keep stirring and shaking the wok at the same, until you acquire the Balti rhythm!

ESSENTIAL BALTI TECHNIQUES

1. TANDOORI MARINADING AND COOKING

A number of Balti recipes use tandoori poultry, lamb or mutton and liver. Although tandoori cuts are available in butchers and supermarkets they come nowhere near the real thing. If you follow this recipe the result will be as close as it's possible to get without the benefit of a tandoor oven.

Prepare in advance if you intend embarking on a Balti spree. Once cooked tandoori or tikka meat is perfect for freezing. The marinade once used may be kept for use once more, but obviously fresh is best!

Tandoori chicken and chicken tikka

(or you can substitute lamb or fish)

1 x 1.4 kg / 3 lb chicken, jointed, or 680 g / 1½ lb chicken breasts, thighs or drumsticks, or 680 g / 1½ lb boned lamb, cut into cubes, or 680 g / 1½ lb fish, cut into large cubes
1 tbsp salt
juice of 2 lemons
300 ml / ½ pint plain yoghurt
4 cm /1½ inch cube of fresh ginger, peeled and grated
2 large garlic cloves, crushed
1 fresh green chilli, finely chopped
palmful of chopped fresh coriander
5 tsp Balti spice mix (page 26)
150 ml / ¼ pint vegetable oil
1 tbsp chopped fresh mint or 1 tsp dried mint
1-1½ tbsp food colouring (optional)

Prepare the day before you need it!

Cut deep slits in the chicken joints and lay them in a single layer in a large dish. (Lamb or fish chunks are laid in a single layer too. It is not necessary to cut slits in the lamb or the fish.) Sprinkle half of the salt and lemon juice over the pieces and rub it in well, making sure it goes deep into the slits. Turn the pieces over and rub in the remaining salt and lemon juice. Set aside for 30 minutes.

Put all the remaining ingredients in a blender or food processor and whizz until you have a runny paste. Pour into a large bowl. Wash off the salt and lemon thoroughly, then add the chicken pieces (or lamb or fish) to the bowl. Make sure that each piece is covered with the paste, including deep in the slits.

Cover the bowl with cling film. Chill at least overnight; 24 hours is good, longer is even better.

Preheat the oven to its maximum setting. Let it heat up for at least 15 minutes, until the stove practically throbs!

Take the chicken pieces out of the marinade one by one, smooth off the tandoori paste and lay them in a single layer in a baking tray. Place this high in the very hot oven and bake for about 25 minutes, pouring off liquid when it accumulates in the bottom of the tray. You may have to do this twice during the cooking time. The finished chicken, lamb or fish should be fairly dry on the surface, moist in the middle. Test the chicken with a fork to see if it is done: the meat should be tender and there should be no hint of pink (with lamb the meat should be still slightly pink in the middle).

Turn the oven off (it will be very relieved!) remove the chicken and allow it to cool.

If there are any bits of roasted marinade left in the bottom of the tray these are what Mr Aslam of Salma's calls 'red masala'. Keep them to one side if you are going to make Salma's Special Balti soon.

When it is cool enough to handle, remove the meat from the bones. Now that it is off-the-bone it is chicken tikka and ready to be used in Balti recipes.

Lamb and fish are cooked in the same way, but lamb will take about 35 minutes and fish 15-20 minutes. Test with a fork. Lamb should still be slightly pink in the middle. Fish should be moist rather than wet, the flakes ready to separate when you test with the fork. If you are cooking smaller quantities, use this basic recipe. Too much won't make any difference. For larger quantities of meat double the marinade ingredients.

You will find alternative tandoori marinades in these recipes:

Spice Valley's Tandoori Steam Chicken Balti (pages 70-71)

Minar's Liver Tikka (page 39)

Nirala's Tandoori Fish (page 41)

Ruby's Lahori Balti (page 97)

Memsahib's Gosht Masala Balti (page 87)

Brick Lane's Sonar Bangla's Lamb Pasanda Balti (page 76)

Boots Cookshops have introduced a tandoori cooking pot. This is an unglazed pot that you use in your oven. It produces deliciously moist meat ideal for use in a Balti. If you want to serve Tandoori chicken or lamb on its own as a starter you might want to crisp it up a little under the grill.

2. PAR-COOKING AND PRE-COOKING AND MAKING BALTI SAUCE

Par-cooking lamb and mutton and making Balti sauce

Many recipes call for meat that has been nearly cooked, to be finished off in the wok. This basic recipe also makes Balti sauce.

900 g / 2 lb boned lamb or mutton, cut into 2.5 cm / 1 inch cubes
2 onions, chopped
3 tbsp vegetable oil
2 small tomatoes, chopped
5 tsp Balti spice mix (page 26)
2 tsp turmeric powder
1/2 fresh green pepper, seeded and chopped
2.5 cm / 1 inch cube fresh ginger, peeled and grated
2 garlic cloves, crushed
1/2 tsp chilli powder
1 tbsp dried methi
1 1/2 tsp salt
1 tsp garam masala (pages 25-26)

Preheat the oven to 200°C / 400°F / gas mark 6.

Fry the onions in the oil in a flame-proof casserole until they are translucent. Add all the other ingredients except the meat, and 300 ml / 1/2 pint of water. Bring to the boil, then add the meat.

Put the casserole in the oven and braise the meat for 45 minutes, checking every 10 minutes or so to give it a stir and make sure there is enough water.

When the meat is tender on the outside but still a little pink in the middle take it out with a slotted spoon and put it to one side. (The meat's cooking will be finished off in the wok.) When the casserole is cool, empty the contents into a blender or food processor and liquidise. This is now your basic Balti sauce. It should be the consistency of thickish soup.

N.B. Mutton will take a little longer to cook than lamb.

You will find other ways to par-cook meat in these recipes:

Adil's Tinda Gosht Balti (page 73)
Sher Khan's Mutton Balti (page 102)
Ruby's Rogon Josh Balti (page 98)
Kababish's Venison Balti (page 83)
Empire's Acharie Meat Balti (page 78)

Pre-cooking chicken and making Balti sauce

Chicken for Balti dishes must be thoroughly cooked, not partly cooked as you do for lamb or mutton.

1 x 1.4 kg / 3 lb chicken, jointed, or use breast and leg pieces
3 onions, chopped
2 tomatoes, chopped
1 tbsp salt
5 cm / 2 inch cube fresh ginger, peeled and grated

6 large garlic cloves, crushed
2¹/2 tsp Balti spice mix (page 26)
1 tsp turmeric powder
4 whole cloves
5 cm / 2 inch cinnamon stick
1 black, or 4 green, cardamoms, broken
   slightly open
2 black peppercorns
1 tbsp chopped fresh coriander
2 tbsp vegetable oil

Put all the ingredients except the coriander and oil into a large saucepan and add 300 ml / ¹/2 pint water. Bring to the boil and stir, then turn the heat to low, cover with a lid and simmer for 30-35 minutes. The chicken is ready when the meat comes cleanly from the bone. Remove the chicken and set it aside.

Add the coriander and oil to the pan and bring back to the boil. Cook, stirring, for 2 minutes. Pour the contents of the pan into your blender or food processor, picking out as you do the cinnamon stick and the cardamom pods (the cloves and peppercorns won't matter). Liquidise this soup and it becomes your Balti sauce, a very good one (as we've commented in our notes!).

When the chicken is cool enough to handle remove and discard the bones, feeling carefully for all the tiny ones. Cut or break the meat into bite-size chunks. You will find another way of pre-cooking chicken and making Balti sauce in the recipe for:

Salma's Special Balti (page 67)
And for simply pre-cooking chicken when you're in a hurry:
   Imran's Murghi Pakora (page 37)
   Ahmed's Chicklama (page 32)

Par-cooking vegetables

Whenever possible we use one saucepan, and add vegetables following a timetable so they all finish at the same time, still with a hint of natural crunch left, ready to be finished off in the wok. This can only be a very rough guide to times; check often to see that they are not over cooking. Use any vegetables you like.

Put a large saucepan with plenty of salted water on the stove. Add any root vegetables – potatoes, carrots or turnips – together with some Balti spice mix and turmeric. Bring to the boil.

Add any other vegetables in this order and at roughly these times:
   after 5 minutes: broccoli, courgettes
   after 3 more minutes: cauliflower, aubergine, peppers
   after 3 more minutes: cabbage
   after 5 more minutes: spinach, ladies' fingers
   Cook for 5 more minutes, then remove from the heat and drain.

The obvious disadvantage of cooking everything at once is that if one vegetable cooks faster than the others it is fiddly to remove and set aside. But it is more convenient than having several pans on the go at the same time.

Pre-cooking chick peas (chana)

Soak the chick peas in water overnight. Put them with their soaking water into a saucepan and bring to the boil. Cover the pan, turn the heat to low and simmer for 1½ hours or until they are tender. Drain, keeping some of their stock if the recipe directs.

Pre-cooking red kidney beans and black eye beans

Put the beans into a pan with water to cover. Bring to the boil, turn the heat down and simmer for 5 minutes. Remove from the heat and let the beans soak for 1 hour.

Bring back to the boil. Cover with a lid, leaving a small gap, and simmer until the beans are tender but still have 'bite': red kidney beans for 1 hour, black eye beans for 20-25 minutes. Drain.

Pre-cooking dal or yellow split peas

Dal can be a dish on its own. In Balti cooking pre-cooked dal is added to a range of meat dishes as well as vegetarian Baltis. So if you're planning a number of Balti extravaganzas cook a big panful of dal and freeze it in portions.

Chana dal is sold in Asian greengrocers and is the one most commonly used in Asian cooking, but yellow split peas are a good substitute and can be found everywhere.

The following recipe serves 4-6 as a dish on its own. You will often need less for adding to a Balti.

225 g / 8 oz chana dal or yellow split peas
½ tsp turmeric powder
¾-1 tsp salt

Put the dal or split peas into a large pan with 1.2 litres / 2 pints water. Bring to the boil and skim off any scum that collects. Add the turmeric. Cover (leaving the lid slightly ajar) and simmer for 1½ hours or until the dal is tender but still has bite. Stir now and then during the last half hour. Add the salt after cooking and stir it in thoroughly.

Portion into servings for 2 or 4, pack into freezer bags and freeze if you're not Balti-ing in the next 3 days.

3. MAKING BALTI SAUCES

Each Balti chef has his own variation on this basic theme. We have seen potatoes added, as well as coconut cream and even dairy cream. Many chefs add a bouquet garni (page 26).

Basic Balti sauce (everyday version)

This quick, easy sauce forms the basis of most recipes in the book.

Makes 750 ml / 1¼ pints

3 tbsp vegetable oil
4 onions, chopped
small piece of fresh ginger, peeled and grated

1 large garlic clove, crushed
1 tomato, chopped
1/2 tsp turmeric powder
1 tsp paprika
1/2 tsp ground cumin
1/2 tsp ground coriander
1/4 tsp chilli powder
salt to taste
palmful of chopped fresh coriander

Heat the oil in a large saucepan over moderate heat and fry the onions, ginger and garlic until the onions are translucent. Add the tomato and stir-fry, breaking it up with the spoon. Pour in 300 ml / 1/2 pint water and stir in the other ingredients. Bring to the boil. Turn the heat to low, cover with a lid and simmer for 30 minutes. Remove from the heat and allow to cool. Pour into a blender or food processor and liquidise.

Balti sauce (Rolls Royce version)

This is an even better sauce – more complex in taste and, of course, to make. The result does justify the little extra time.

Makes 1 litre / 1³/4 pints

3 tbsp vegetable oil
2 cm / ³/4 inch cube fresh ginger, peeled and grated
1 large garlic clove, crushed
5 onions, chopped
4 tomatoes, chopped
2 tsp ground coriander

1 tsp ground cumin
1/2 tsp turmeric powder
1/4 tsp chilli powder
1/2 tsp paprika
1/2 tsp garam masala
2 bay leaves
4 brown cardamoms, broken slightly open
1¹/2 tsp dried methi
1¹/2 tsp salt

Heat the oil in a large saucepan over moderate heat. Put in the ginger and garlic and stir. Add the onions and stir-fry until they are translucent. Pour in 250 ml / 9 fl oz water and bring to the boil. Add the tomatoes and all the spices, including the bay leaves, cardamoms and methi, and the salt. Cover the pan, turn the heat to low and simmer for 30 minutes.

Remove the bay leaves and cardamom pods and liquidise the rest.

Two more, very specific Balti sauces can be found in the recipes for:
    Royal Al-Faisal's Keema Karela Balti
        (page 93)
    Istafa's Murghi Makhani Balti (page 54)

4. MAKING SPICE MIXES

Garam masalas should be made in small quantities. Don't store them for too long: freshly ground is best.

A really good garam masala

Makes 2 tbsp
1¹/2 tbsp black peppercorns

*3/4 tbsp black cumin seeds, or use ordinary
  cumin seeds*
1¹/2 tsp whole cloves
4 large brown cardamom pods
5 cm / 2 inch cinnamon stick
1/2 whole nutmeg
*2 star anise (optional) (Star anise is one of
  the mystery ingredients used by some of
  the more secretive Balti chefs.)*

Gently roast all the spices and grind
everything to a fine powder in a coffee
grinder. Store in a tightly lidded small jar,
out of direct sunlight.

A more basic garam masala

Makes 4 tsp
16 black peppercorns
12 green cardamoms
8 whole cloves
1 tsp ground cinnamon

Roast and grind to a fine powder in a
coffee grinder.

An emergency garam masala

Makes 2 tbsp
12 green cardamoms
2 dried bay leaves
1 tbsp ground coriander
2 tsp ground cumin
1 tsp ground cinnamon

Grind the cardamoms and bay leaves and
mix with the dry spices.

Balti spice mix

Makes 5 tsp
2 tsp paprika
1¹/2 tsp ground coriander
3/4 tsp ground cumin
1/2 tsp salt
1/4 tsp chilli powder

Stir the spices together until evenly mixed.

Bouquet garni

5 whole cloves
8 black peppercorns
4 cm / 1¹/2 inch cinnamon stick
2 bay leaves
3 brown cardamoms, broken slightly open
1 tsp cumin seeds
1 tbsp coriander seeds

Cut a piece of clean muslin about 15 cm /
6 inches square. Place all the spices on it
and tie it up securely into a little parcel.
When the spices have done their job of
infusing flavour you can remove them
easily.

BALTI ACCOMPANIMENTS

To get your taste buds revved up for the
main course, restaurants serve a more-ish
Balti dip (see the top recipe on page 145).
It's yoghurt and mint based, takes no time
at all to make, and is served in individual
china dishes. You dip your poppadoms
into it.

DRINKS TO SERVE WITH BALTIS

Most people seem to prefer ice-cold beers and lagers with spicy food, believing long, cool drinks to be the antidote to the sting in the tail of the green chilli. But a variety of wines go down a treat with Balti dishes too. So do long, non-alcoholic drinks traditional to the indigenous country. Just like the food itself, anything goes. Feel your way around and discover what you like best.

Beer

Since alcohol is proscribed by the Koran, there is no tradition of drinking alcohol with Karahi dishes. However, no such restrictions apply to Birmingham's Balti enthusiasts, so if you hanker after the authenticity that could have been, it makes sense to consider the widely available Indian beers, Cobra White Label and Kingfisher.

Cobra is the less alcoholic (4.4% as opposed to 5.2%) and has more quaffable freshness. This may be because Kingfisher is now brewed under license in the UK and seems to have suffered the blandification that so often separates a UK brewed beer from the original.

Other widely available Asian beers are Tiger from Singapore and Singha from Thailand. If you have specialist West Indian shops nearby, look out for Carib, brewed in Trinidad and preferable to Jamaica's ubiquitous (UK brewed) Red Stripe. Recommended from Europe are Italy's Nastro Azurro and Spain's San Miguel.

If you want to move away from blonde beers, sample Coopers Sparkling Ale from Australia. That's not to forget canned draught Guinness. If you live near a real specialist off-license and can take your beer spicy hot as well as ice-cold ask them about Crazy Al's Chili Beer from Texas or Crazy Ed's brewed in Cave Creek, Arizona, with a green chilli in every bottle. At the other end of the scale there's the sublimely refreshing Corsaire from the Lorraine brewery on the French Caribbean island of Martinique.

If you really want to show off, search out Mickey's Strong Lager from La Crosse, Wisconsin or Pig's Eye Pilsner brewed in Minnesota. High altitude Andes Cerveza is bound to get any occasion off to a flying start, and if you really want to be weird try Irish Potato Ale.

It's also worth bearing in mind your duty free allowances when in France. It's extremely cheap to pick up a 'slab' of 25 cl bottles of the universally available Kanterbrau, recently voted best French supermarket beer in the prestigious Gault-Millau Magazine.

In Birmingham, Banks is favourite for a Balthouse evening out. Banks' Wolverhampton and Dudley Brewery is the presence felt in 95% of the pubs in the Black Country. Their slogan is 'unspoilt by progress'. Banks is available in cans at off-licences as Mild, Bitter, Old and Strong Ales. Another beer that has rapidly been adopted by Balti enthusiasts is Manchester-brewed creamy Boddingtons.

Wines

White wine

There is a contender from India. Surprising as it may sound Omar Khayam, made near Bombay with the help of the Piper Heidsieck French champagne house, is worth looking for. It's variable, but at its best can be an excellent way to warm up your guests at under a tenner a bottle.

The natural acidity of spiced food will overwhelm many classic white wines. Instead go for well chilled Alsace Gewürtztraminer - the lychee-like fruit complements Balti dishes well. You may also safely drink almost any Australian Riesling. Don't turn your nose up at the thought - Australian Riesling is uncompromisingly dry and will surprise you with its ability to partner many of these dishes. Three suggestions for contrasting, rather than complementary wines: if you want the classic 'dry white' you could do worse than Chardonnay Vin de Pays D'Oc made by Hugh Ryman, available at Sainsbury's. You might also enjoy the hugely oakey, smoky white Rioja from the Maques de Murrieta called 'Ygay'. Another Spanish contender is the melony Vin Esmaralda by Miguel Torres.

Rosé

Not strictly a rosé, but a natural complement for this food is Australian Sparkling Shiraz. Particularly recommended is the 1987 Seppelt Sparkling Shiraz, available at Oddbins. Also, Mumm Cuvée Napa, a remarkable strawberry tasting sparkling wine from California's Napa Valley. A refined rosé for partnering fish Baltis is Château de Sours 1990, a rosé Bordeaux made by an Englishman and currently generating huge excitement as the world's best rosé. Other rosés that are well-rounded enough are France's Tavel, or Cune Rioja Rosada, from Spain.

Red wine

Red wines that can take a good chilling and come out fighting: southern French reds like Corbières, Minervoise, Côteaux de Languedoc or even Fitou. As a general rule forget Italian wines except possibly a light and chilled Valpolicella or Veneto Cabernet Franc. Forget all Bordeaux's clarets, which were designed for a different role in life. Beaujolais, either in its generic form or one of the cru Beaujolais like a Brouilly or Moulin-à-Vent should provide excellent drinking with Baltis as will an American challenger for Beaujolais' grapey quaffability, called J. Lohr Wildflower Gamay - once again from Oddbins.

Reds at room temperature might not be a natural choice, but you will find Rhône wines stand up best, from generic Côtes-du-Rhône through to St-Joseph and Côte-Rôtie.

Two personal favourites that have the

kind of huge, assertive quality to hold their own in any Baltihouse: Château Musar, a unique and delicious red from the B'Kaa valley in Lebanon (Marks & Spencer are selling a lighter wine from the same vineyard - Hochar); and the remarkable Napa Valley blend of odd grape varieties called Nero Misto, by Elyse as far as I know, only from Bibendum in London.

Traditional non-alcoholic drinks

These range from mango crushes to cooling sweet or salt 'lassis'. You'll find the recipes on pages 148-50.

BALTI NAAN AND CHAPATI

As we have mentioned Balti is never eaten with rice, only with bread. The most common in Baltihouses is naan, a leavened bread that is fluffy, flat and often pear-drop shaped. In Baltihouses the naan to accompany the Balti is as important as the dish itself. Forget the trifling little pieces you've eaten in Indian restaurants. For group or family outings naan can be anything from pillow-sized to maximum-tog-duvet-sized!

Traditionally they are cooked at high temperature in a tandoor - a large chimney-shaped oven lined with clay. A real pillow is sometimes used for the largest naan to spare the chef's fingers when he presses the dough to the inside surface. These light, fluffy extravaganzas are baked plain or studded with seeds or slices of garlic, stuffed with spicy vegetables, meat or even dried fruits and nuts.

You can buy naan and its unleavened relative the chapati in most supermarkets, but both are infinitely nicer when you make them yourself. The best way of baking naan without a tandoor is to use a tava – a flat circular cast-iron implement with a wooden handle. You can get a tava really hot on the stove and transfer it easily to the grill for the final few moments. Tavas can be found at Asian suppliers or through our own mail order house (page 157). Alternatively, you could use a heavy baking tray or frying pan, a hot oven and a hot grill. Recipes for naan and chapati are on pages 143-4.

BALTI SWEETS AND DESSERTS

No Balti meal is complete (if you've got the room) without a Balti pudding. Many Baltihouses have the words 'Sweet Centre' above the door, or a little shop next door where you can pick your own or take away for later. Kulfi and Barfi are two of the favourites. Kulfi is an exotic version of ice-cream and Barfi is closest to a light fudge. Both are made very simply with fresh or evaporated milk subtly flavoured with spices. They come in vivid colours and enticing flavours.

STARTERS

ADIL'S STUFFED GREEN CHILLI BHAJI
(Manager and Chef Mr Ashiraf)

So simple, and quite impressive. Dare your guests try a starter of green chillies? It is surprisingly not too hot at all: these big 'bullet' chillies are reasonably mild.

4 Stages • Medium • Serves 4

8 big fresh green chillies (about 15 cm / 6 inches long)
450 g / 1 lb potatoes
salt
3 tbsp vegetable oil, plus more for deep-frying

1 tsp whole mustard seeds
3 garlic cloves, finely chopped
freshly ground black pepper
115 g / 4 oz gram flour
1 egg
pinch of garam masala (page 25)

Stage 1: Making the stuffing
Peel and wash the potatoes, then cook in boiling salted water. When they are just done drain and let them cool a little. Cut them into 1 cm / 1/2 inch cubes.

Heat the 3 tablespoons of vegetable oil in a frying pan over moderate heat. When it is hot put in the mustard seeds. When they start to pop add the garlic. Stir until it starts to brown. Put the potatoes in and stir them around to cover them with the oil. Sprinkle with salt and grind lots of black pepper over them. Stir thoroughly. Turn the heat to low, cover the pan and let the potatoes cook gently for about 5 minutes.

Stir finally to make sure all the pieces of potato are covered with the spiced oil. Remove from the heat and leave them to cool.

Stage 2: Stuffing the chillies
Make a slit in each of the chillies, big enough to stuff them through but without breaking them apart. Remove the seeds. Rub a little salt inside and set them aside for about 20 minutes.

When the potatoes are cool enough to handle, carefully stuff them into the chillies. Do this loosely so that the chillies don't split completely, or lose their shape.

Stage 3: Making a batter
Sift the gram flour and a pinch of salt into a bowl. Beat in the egg. Add a little ground pepper, the garam masala and enough water to make a thick porridgey batter.

Stage 4: Frying the chillies
Heat a large pan of oil for deep frying. Dip the chillies into the batter, and deep fry for about 3 minutes. When cooked the batter will be smooth and golden, the chillies still slightly crunchy to the bite. Drain on kitchen paper, then serve.

AHMED'S CHICKLAMA STARTER
(Proprietor and Chef Mr Ahmed)

These are delicious round patties made of naan dough, filled with spicy chicken and deep-fried. Katlama is the classic minced meat version. Use 680 g / 1¹/₂ lb of the mince mixture from Chapli Kebabs (page 34).

3 Stages • Medium • Serves 4

*1 small chicken, skinned and meat
   removed
4 tbsp vegetable oil, plus more for deep
   frying
3 garlic cloves, crushed*

*2 tsp cumin seeds
2 onions, chopped
2 tsp curry powder
dough to make 3 naans (page 143)
oil for frying*

Stage 1: Frying the chicken

Heat the 4 tablespoons of oil in a wok over moderately high heat and stir-fry the garlic and cumin seeds for 1 minute. Add the onions and fry until they are soft. Add the curry powder and the chicken meat and stir-fry for 20 minutes or until the chicken is tender.

Remove from the heat and allow to cool. Cut or tear the chicken into small pieces.

Stage 2: Making the chicklamas

Divide the dough into 4 balls. Flatten each one into a disc. Divide the chicken mixture among the discs. Fold in the sides to cover the filling and mould into round patties about 1 cm / ¹/₂ inch thick. Make a hole right through the middle of each to let steam escape.

Stage 3: Frying the chicklamas

Heat a pan of oil for deep-frying. Test the heat by dropping in a cube of bread. It should brown in about 40 seconds. Deep-fry the chicklamas for 2 minutes. Drain on kitchen paper.

Serve with Ahmed's Balti dip (page 145).

BRICK LANE'S SONAR BANGLA'S CAPSICUM DELIGHT

(Proprietors Mr Sahid and Emdadul Hoque, Chef Mr T. Miah)

One of London's very own Baltihouses serves an unusual and delicious starter, a spicy stuffed green pepper. We were intrigued at the unique use of sardine in the stuffing!

3 Stages • Medium hot • Serves 4

*4 large green peppers, de-capped at stalk
    end and seeded*
vegetable oil for deep frying
1 large onion, chopped
4 tbsp butter or vegetable ghee
4 garlic cloves, finely chopped
1 tsp salt

5 tsp Balti spice mix (page 26)
1 tbsp tomato purée
2 ladles of Balti sauce
1 tbsp dried methi
3 tbsp chopped fresh coriander
4 x 120 g cans sardines in tomato sauce

Stage 1: Making the Balti sauce

See page 24.

Stage 2: Deep frying the peppers

Heat the oil in a large pan until it is very hot. Test it by flicking water on the surface; it is the right temperature when it sizzles.

Deep fry the peppers for 7 minutes, or until they are soft and the skin begins to bubble. Remove them from the oil, shaking off any residue. Keep warm.

Stage 3: Stuffing the peppers

Chop the caps you have removed from the peppers and mix with the chopped onion.

In a frying pan heat the butter and fry the garlic until it starts to brown. Add the onion and chopped peppers and stir-fry until translucent. Add the salt, Balti spice mix and tomato purée. Stir-fry, shaking the wok, for 8-10 minutes.

Add the Balti sauce, methi and coriander and finally the sardines. Stir and break up the sardines with the spoon. Turn the heat down and simmer for 10 more minutes.

Remove from the heat and carefully stuff each of the peppers with the spicy fish filling. Serve upside down, with a small mixed salad.

CHANNI'S CHAPLI KEBAB STARTER

(Proprietor and Chef Mr 'Channi' Dogra)

A chapli (which means 'slipper') is like a spicy hamburger. It's not skewered.

2 Stages • Spicy but not hot • Ideal for a barbecue • Serves 4

340 g / ¾ lb minced lamb, minced again
   in a food processor
1 green pepper, seeded and chopped
1 red pepper, seeded and chopped
2 small onions, very finely chopped
1 tomato, finely chopped
½ tsp cumin seeds
2 tsp chopped fresh coriander

½ tsp crushed garlic
½ tsp grated fresh ginger
1 fresh green chilli, very finely chopped
½ tsp salt
¼ tsp garam masala (page 25)
juice of ½ lemon
1 tbsp gram flour
1 litre / 1¾ pints vegetable oil for deep frying

Stage 1: Making the kebabs

Mix together the peppers, onions, tomato, cumin seeds and chopped coriander. In another bowl combine the minced lamb with the garlic, ginger, green chilli, salt, garam masala and lemon juice, squeezing and kneading to mix well.

Add the spiced meat to the fresh ingredients and sprinkle the gram flour on top. Wet your hands to stop the mixture sticking to them and mix, squeezing and punching, until it is evenly blended.

Divide the meat mixture into 4 equal lumps. Wet your hands and mould into oval hamburgers about 1 cm / ½ inch thick.

Stage 2: Frying the kebabs

In a large wok heat the vegetable oil until it just sizzles when you sprinkle a little water into it. Using a fish slice slide one kebab in gently. After 4 minutes slip the next one in. After another 3 minutes remove the first one and gently slide in the third. As you take them out put the kebabs on a wire rack to drain, and keep hot. Repeat the process once more until the four are done. During this deep frying remove any loose bits so they don't burn and make the oil 'bad', as Channi puts it.

Serve the kebabs with chopped lettuce and sliced tomato and onion, plus cucumber if you like it. Sprinkle a little very finely chopped coriander over the kebabs. Add a spoonful of Balti dip (page 145) to each plate. For the final perfect touch put a little dollop of thick Imli sauce (page 146) beside the Balti dip.

Note: Chapli kebabs are even nicer barbecued. Cook as you would hamburgers.

THE BALTIHOUSE KITCHEN MAIL ORDER SERVICE

To serve Balti dishes at home you need the traditional Balti bowls or Karahi and the range of spices used in most Balti meals. If you're cooking for four you can either stir-fry the Balti in a large wok and serve sizzling in individual Balti bowls or cook each Balti in its individual Karahi. We offer a beginner's pack for two people with eight different spices or spice mixes. This way you can achieve the traditional taste in the authentic way.

The kit includes:

2 x 10" Balti bowls

Repeated stir-frying achieves the non-stick black patina famous in Balti circles.

1 naan basket

Made from woven coloured straw and essential for serving a stack of naan bread or wafer-thin chapatis. Connoisseurs never eat rice with a Balti.

2 specially ground and blended Balti spice mixes sealed to retain freshness

Usually only available through Baltihouses, our Balti Spice Mix, and Garam Masala which is home roasted and ground.

Balti Spice Mix (100gms)

Garam Masala (50gms)

6 Balti spices in sealed packets

Chilli powder (50gms)

Adds fire to your Balti.

Haldi (Turmeric) powder (50gms)

Adds a saffron-like colour to vegetables - essential for making dal.

Brown Elaichi (Cardamoms) (50gms)

Broken open slightly, cardamoms give a delicate flavour to savoury dishes.

Ground Jeera (Cumin) (50gms)

Gives that authentic Asian flavour - indispensable in Balti cooking.

Ground Dhania (Coriander) (50gms)

Enhances the flavour of both vegetables and meat.

Methi (Fenugreek) leaves (25g)

One of the well-kept secrets that distinguishes Balti from ordinary curry.

Price £25.99 including p&p.

Each pack comes with instructions on how to care for your Balti bowls.

Further Baltihouse Kit & Caboodle is available, including a Tava, a flat pan for cooking naan and chapatis, and order forms for more spices including the exotic ones. Details will be sent on request or with your order.
'100 Best Balti Curries' by Diane Lowe & Mike Davidson, published by Pavilion available from good bookshops.

Please send .... Baltihouse Kitchen Kits at £25.99 each.
Total cost £.................. I enclose cheque for the full amount.

Signature ....

Name ....

Address ....

....

.... Postcode ....

Post to: Baltihouse Kitchen, PO Box 4401
HENLEY-ON-THAMES, Oxon RG9 1FW.

Fifty of Birmingham's most famous Baltihouses shared their recipe secrets with us over a long, sometimes arduous, but always delicious three years. It was the first time any Baltihouse recipe had ever been written down or shared with anyone outside the chef's immediate family. We watched the chefs at work and got to know how they roast and grind their own distinctive blend of spices. They helped us prepare recipes for a family of four, from the very simple to the more complex. The result is the 100 Best Balti Curries - Authentic Dishes from the Baltihouses compiled by Diane Lowe and Mike Davidson. Now for the first time everyone can cook their favourite Balti from around 50 top Baltihouses. And if you've yet to try one, you've got a real treat in store, just by following our simple recipes.

To help you cook Balti in the authentic Baltihouse way we're offering all the kit and caboodle the chefs use to cook and serve their famous Baltis and the spices used to create that special Balti taste.

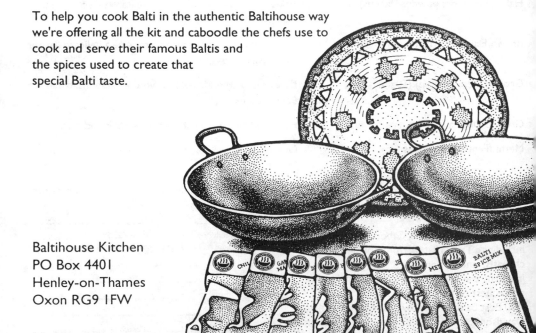

Baltihouse Kitchen
PO Box 4401
Henley-on-Thames
Oxon RG9 1FW

DIWAN'S RESHMI KEBAB STARTER
(Proprietor and Chef Mr Uddin)

A kebab made of minced chicken. It makes an appetizing starter or is excellent as a summer barbecue titbit.

2 Stages • Gently spiced • Serves 4

450 g / 1 lb minced chicken
1 onion, finely chopped
2 cm / 3/4 inch cube fresh ginger, peeled and grated

1 tsp ground cumin
2 tsp ground coriander
1/2 tsp garam masala (page 25)
2 tsp chopped fresh coriander

Stage 1: Making the kebabs
Put all the ingredients into a bowl and mash well by hand. Mould into sausage shapes, about 2 cm / 3/4 inch thick and 15 cm / 6 inches long, around barbecue skewers.

Stage 2: Cooking the kebabs
Cook under a grill or, better still, on the barbecue. Check often by breaking one open a little with a fork to see when they are cooked.

Serve with a small salad and Balti dip (page 145).

THE EMPIRE'S BALTI FRIED KING PRAWN
(Proprietors Fahim Akhtar and Aslam Perviaz who is also Chef)

Mr Perviaz' dishes have the bold simplicity of haute cuisine. This has a wonderful hot 'toffee-like' dry sauce, all the spices working in tune with each other. It would make an impressive starter for the Big Balti Occasion or a dinner party.

3 Stages • Medium hot • Serves 4

20 raw king prawns
2 tbsp sugar
2 tbsp white malt vinegar
*3 small heads of garlic (yes, whole heads!),
    peeled and chopped*

2 fresh green chillies, chopped
*2 tsp Maggi liquid seasoning, or use
    1 1/2 tsp soy sauce and 1/2 tsp Marmite*
*450 ml / 3/4 pint vegetable oil, plus 5 tbsp
    for the Balti stage*

Stage 1: Cleaning the prawns
Remove the heads and legs but leave the prawns in their shells. Rinse the prawns in warm water.

Add the sugar and vinegar to a bowl of water. Swish the prawns around in this, then leave them to soak for 20 minutes. Remove, and pat dry with kitchen paper.

Stage 2: Marinading the prawns
Drop the garlic and chillies into a food processor. Add the Maggi liquid seasoning, or soy sauce and Marmite, and the 450 ml/ 3/4 pint of oil. Grind to a paste. Put this into a bowl.

Add the prawns to the bowl. Stir, making sure that each prawn is covered with the marinade. Leave for 2 hours.

Stage 3: Balti method
Heat the 5 tablespoons of oil in a large wok over a low heat. Add the king prawns and the marinade. Stir gently, then cover the wok and cook for 2 minutes. Remove the prawns, keep warm, then fry the marinade until it looks like a dark brown textured toffee. Serve the prawns on a bed of fried marinade. Await the compliments!

IMRAN'S MURGHI (CHICKEN) PAKORA STARTER
(Proprietor and Chef Mr Butt)

Traditionally these uneven shaped pieces of chicken, made ever more uneven by the bubbling of the batter in deep frying, are bright orange in colour. You can leave out the food colouring if you prefer. Serve piping hot as a starter or snack with Balti dip (page 145).

3 Stages • Mild • Serves 4

*4 chicken breasts, boned and each cut into
    6 or 8 pieces*
4 cm / 1¹/₂ inch cinnamon stick
2 black cardamoms, broken slightly open
6 whole cloves
8 black peppercorns
1 bay leaf
¹/₂ tsp salt
vegetable oil for deep frying

FOR THE BATTER:
175 g / 6 oz gram flour
¹/₂ tsp salt
¹/₂ tsp garam masala (page 25)
¹/₂ tsp chilli powder
¹/₂ tsp ground ginger
¹/₂ tsp garlic powder
*orange or yellow food colouring
    (optional)*

Stage 1: Pre-cooking the chicken

Put the chicken pieces into a saucepan with enough water to cover them by about 1 cm / ¹/₂ inch. Add the cinnamon, cardamoms, cloves, peppercorns, bay leaf and salt. Bring to the boil. Turn the heat to low and simmer for 15-20 minutes or until the chicken is just cooked. Add more water if necessary. Drain the chicken; discard all the spices.

Stage 2: Making the batter

Sift the flour into a bowl and add the salt, garam masala, chilli powder, ground ginger and garlic powder. Stir to mix. Gradually stir in enough water (175–225 ml / 6–8 fl oz) to make a smooth batter that is the consistency of porridge. Add a few drops of food colouring if you are using it. Let the batter stand for 30 minutes.

Stage 3: Frying the pakoras

Put the chicken pieces into the batter and stir them around, making sure that each piece is well covered.

Heat oil in a deep pan until a small cube of stale bread dropped in turns golden in about 1 minute. Lower the chicken pieces, a few at a time, into the hot oil and fry for 3–4 minutes or until crisp. If the oil should get too hot remove from the heat for a few minutes. Lift the pakoras from the oil and drain on kitchen paper.

Serve immediately.

KIRRAN'S FISH STARTER
(Proprietor and Chef Mr Abdul Hafeez)

This is such an easy dish to make. It consists of a yoghurt and spice marinade and the fish is then fried. Eat as a starter or snack. It's even good cold!

2 Stages • Medium • Serves 4

680 g / 1¹/₂ lb silver hake, skinned, boned
   and cut into pieces
1 tbsp ground ginger
1 tbsp garlic powder
450 ml / ³/₄ pint plain yoghurt

1 tbsp chilli powder
2 tsp salt
1¹/₂ tbsp ground coriander
8-10 tbsp vegetable oil for frying

Stage 1: Marinading the fish
(If possible, do this the day before cooking.) Put the fish pieces into a bowl and sprinkle the ginger and garlic powder over them. Toss the pieces and make sure all are covered. Pour in the yoghurt and stir that around, then add the chilli powder, salt and coriander. Stir it all, making sure the marinade covers all the fish. Cover with cling film and leave in the fridge overnight.

If you want to eat the fish the same day, a couple of hours in the marinade will do.

Stage 2: Frying the fish
Heat the oil in a frying pan on a moderate flame. Take the pieces of fish out of the bowl, bringing as much marinade as you can to the frying pan. Fry the pieces for 5 minutes on each side.

Serve with a small salad and Balti dip (page 145).

MINAR'S LIVER TIKKA STARTER
(Proprietors the Mohammed brothers, Chef M. Sohel)

Tikka-ed lamb's liver makes a stunning starter. The tikka flavour is like a spicy extension of the liver taste itself. Serve this as a starter or as a lunchtime or evening snack with a Balti dip (page 145) and side salad.

2 stages • Hot • Serves 4-6

900 g / 2 lb lamb's liver
500 ml / 18 fl oz plain yoghurt
1½ tbsp dried crushed chillies
2 tbsp tandoori masala powder

1 tsp concentrated mint sauce
2 tsp lemon juice
1 tsp salt

Stage 1: Marinading the liver

Thoroughly rinse the liver, drain and dry with kitchen paper. Cut into 4 cm / 1½ inch pieces. Put the liver in a non-metallic dish large enough to lay the pieces side by side. In a bowl mix together the yoghurt, chillies, tandoori masala, mint sauce, lemon juice and salt. Rub well into the liver. Cover with cling film and marinade for at least 2 hours, longer if possible.

Stage 2: Grilling the liver kebabs

Preheat the grill to maximum. Thread the pieces of liver on to kebab skewers. Grill for about 1 minute on each side. This length of time will give you liver with a pink centre. If you prefer your meat well done, grill for longer.

Serve immediately.

MOKHAM'S GARLIC ALOO (POTATO) TIKKI STARTER

(Proprietors 'Naz' and 'Kal', Chef 'Mr Q' Qayoum)

'Tikki' means round (as opposed to 'tikka' which means skewered). These are delicious, spicy vegetarian croquettes. Rice flour makes for crispness without rising but seems only to be available from Chinese supermarkets. That's where Mr Q gets his, anyway!

2 Stages • Mild • A simple starter • Serves 4

3 large potatoes, boiled and mashed
1 tbsp garlic powder
1 tsp salt
2/3 tsp chilli powder
1 tsp dried methi
1/2 tsp ground cumin
1 tsp ground coriander
2 ladles of rice flour
2 tsp chopped fresh coriander
oil for deep frying

Stage 1: Making the tikki

Mix together all the ingredients except the oil. Shape into 4-5 cm / 1½-2 inch balls. Flatten these to make cakes about 1 cm / ½ inch thick.

Stage 2: Frying the tikki

In a deep saucepan heat the oil on a moderately high flame until it is frying temperature. Test the heat by dropping a cube of bread in; it should brown in about 40 seconds.

Lower the tikki in gently a few at a time. Deep-fry them for 2-3 minutes. Remove and drain them on kitchen paper. Repeat until all the tikki are cooked.

Reheat the oil until it is very hot again and then fry all the tikki a second time. This double frying makes the outsides crisp, while the inside stays soft.

Drain and serve while still warm, with Balti dip (page 145).

NIRALA'S TANDOORI FISH STARTER
(Proprietor Mr Aslam, Chef Mr Asif)

Not having a tandoor oven we were delighted to hear Mr Asif say that shallow frying gives much better flavour. Like all tandoori recipes it involves a long marinade. Another example of a secret garam masala recipe, in this case Mr Asif's mother's secret, containing '2 or 3 spices specially imported from Pakistan'. In respect to her we make sure ours is freshly ground.

2 Stages • Mild • A simple and impressive starter • Serves 4

680 g / 1½ lb silver hake, boned, skinned and cut into pieces
450 ml / ¾ pint plain yoghurt
1½ tsp salt
1 tsp chilli powder
1 tsp ground ginger

of 6 hours. Overnight is best.
¾ tsp garlic powder
1 tsp garam masala, freshly ground (page 25)
1 tbsp red food colouring (optional)
vegetable oil for frying

Stage 1: Marinading the fish
Put the fish in a shallow dish. Mix together all the remaining ingredients, except the oil. Pour over the fish, making sure that the marinade covers the fish completely. Allow to stand for a minimum

Stage 2: Frying the fish
Shallow-fry the fish in hot oil for 5-7 minutes on each side. Serve immediately, while still moist, and accompany with a small salad.

PANJAB TANDOORI'S PANEER PAKORA STARTER
(Proprietor and Chef Kailash Watts)

Paneer is an easy-to-make soft cheese that doesn't melt in cooking. These pakoras are cubes of paneer in a chick pea flour batter, deep-fried. They have the texture of toasted marshmallow and are absolutely delicious.

3 Stages • Gently spiced • A vegetarian starter • Serves 4

600 ml / 1 pint milk
1 tbsp lemon juice
1 tsp mango powder (amchur),
   optional
1 tsp ground cumin
vegetable oil for deep frying

FOR THE BATTER:
170 g / 6 oz gram flour
2 tsp salt
1/4 tsp turmeric powder
1 tsp garam masala (page 25)
1/4 tsp chilli powder

Stage 1: Making the paneer

Bring the milk slowly to the boil in a large saucepan, stirring gently. When it starts to rise stir in the lemon juice. Continue stirring until all the milk curdles. Remove from the heat and allow to cool.

Place a large strainer over a saucepan. Line it with a fine cloth such as muslin. Drain the cooled curdled milk, pressing out the excess liquid (whey).

Lift the cloth containing the curds out of the strainer and place it on a wooden board on the draining board. Press out the curds by hand into a square about 1 cm / 1/2 inch thick. Set a heavy weight, such as a saucepan full of water, on top of the curds and leave for 1 1/2-2 hours.

Cut the compressed paneer into 4 cm / 1 1/2 inch squares.

Stage 2: Making the batter

Sift the flour and salt into a mixing bowl.

Gradually stir in enough water to make a smooth pouring batter. Let it stand for 30 minutes. Add the turmeric, garam masala and chilli powder just before you use the batter.

Stage 3: Frying the pakoras

Slice each square of paneer horizontally, not cutting all the way through, to make into a hinged sandwich. Mix the mango powder and ground cumin. Sprinkle some of the spice mixture inside each sandwich. Close it and dust the outside with the spice mixture too.

Heat a large saucepan of oil to frying temperature. Test by dropping in a cube of bread; it should brown in 60 seconds.

Dip the squares of paneer into the batter a few at a time and lower them into the hot oil. When they are golden brown remove them and drain. Serve while still warm with Imli sauce (page 146).

PARIS'S BARBECUE SHEEKH (MINCED LAMB) KEBABS

(Proprietor Mr Armzan, Partner Farid (John), Chef M Nazir)

Taking food to a barbecue party is always a gamble. This will be very popular and you are unlikely to get any for yourself! So be selfish and cook it on your own barbecue, just for you and a few selected friends!

2 stages • Quite hot • Serves 4-6

900 g / 2 lb minced lamb
small piece of fresh ginger, peeled and
*   grated*
2 garlic cloves, crushed
3/4-1 tsp chilli powder

1/2 tsp garam masala (page 25)
1/2 tsp tandoori masala powder
1 tbsp chopped fresh coriander
little beaten egg to bind

Stage 1: Making the meat mixture
Mix all the ingredients together really well. Chill for 30 minutes.

Stage 2: Shaping and grilling the kebabs
Mould the meat mixture around barbecue skewers to make sausage-shaped kebabs about 2 cm / 3/4 inch thick and about 15 cm / 6 inches long. Grill over charcoal, or under the grill.

N.B. Any of the tandoori marinaded meats would make ideal barbecue subjects.

PREET PALACE'S BHUNA PRAWN AND PUREE

(Proprietor Mr Mittel, Chef Mr Sajjad)

A Baltihouse version of the spring roll, these have a wonderfully sour peppery flavour, not too hot; the family will love them.

3 Stages • Medium hot • Serves 4

225 g / 1/2 lb small peeled cooked prawns
115 g / 4 oz chapati or wholemeal flour
vegetable oil for deep frying, plus 8 tbsp for
    the Balti stage
1/2 green pepper, seeded and finely chopped
2 tsp salt
4 cm / 11/2 inch cube fresh ginger, peeled
    and grated

5 large garlic cloves, crushed
2 tbsp Balti spice mix (page 26)
3/4 tsp Worcestershire sauce
11/2 tbsp tomato purée
2 tomatoes, chopped
4 ladles of Balti sauce

Stage 1: Making the chapatis

Use the flour and 150 ml / 1/4 pint water to make 4 chapatis (page 144) about 20 cm / 8 inches in diameter. (Or you can use 4 shop-bought chapatis. Deep fry them in hot oil, one at a time, for 20-30 seconds each. They will be soft, like heavy silk. Drain on kitchen paper and place on a wire rack to cool.

Stage 2: Making the Balti sauce

See page 24.

Stage 3: Balti method

Chef Sajjad works very fast, the pan on fire for half the time. Work as fast as you dare: the less time on the heat the 'cleaner' the Balti will look and taste.

Heat the 8 tablespoons of oil in a large wok. Fry the prawns, green pepper, ginger and garlic until soft. Stir and shake the wok throughout the whole Balti process whenever you aren't actually adding ingredients. Add 11/2 teaspoons of the salt (use the rest later to adjust the seasoning), the spice mix and the Worcestershire sauce. Put the tomato purée and tomatoes in and pour the Balti sauce over everything. Stir violently and break the tomato pieces up with the spoon. Leave the heat fairly high and, still stirring, dry the mixture off for about 3–4 minutes.

Spread one of the chapatis on a flat surface. When the Balti mixture is just cool enough to handle, spoon one-quarter of it on to the chapati. Fold into a tidy parcel, tucking in the ends neatly. Do the other three and serve on side plates with a slice of lemon, a little shredded lettuce and a slice each of cucumber and tomato.

Eat while still warm using your fingers.

SALMA'S PAKORA STARTER
(Proprietors Mr Ali and Mr Aslam, who is also Chef)

Both of the partners worked for many years for the Post Office and, reflecting their passion for food, retired early to open Salma's, an anagram of Mr Aslam's name. This is unlikely to be a coincidence: he is the extrovert of the partnership!

These pakoras are ideal as cocktail snacks, or as a starter. The children will love them and will have to be rationed! The more knobbly and un-uniform in shape the more authentically Asian they look. Mr Aslam reminds us the smaller the pieces the faster they cook.

3 Stages • Mildly spiced • Serves 4-6

450 g / 1 lb potatoes, peeled and cut into
*   2 cm / 3/4 inch pieces*
225 g / 8 oz gram flour or plain flour
1 1/2 tsp salt
1/2 tsp chilli powder
1/2 tsp ground coriander
1/2 tsp ground cumin
1/2 tsp ground cardamom
1/2 tsp ground cinnamon
1/2 tsp ground cloves

1/2 tsp baking powder
450 g / 1 lb onions, chopped or sliced into
*   rings*
225 g / 1/2 lb fresh spinach, cooked,
*   drained and chopped, or use frozen*
*   spinach, thawed and drained*
optional additions or substitutes:
*   aubergine pieces, mushrooms or*
*   cauliflower florets*
vegetable oil for deep frying

Stage 1: Par-cooking the potatoes
Cook the potatoes in boiling salted water for 10 minutes. Drain and set aside.

Stage 2: Making the mixture
Sift the flour into a large mixing bowl. Mix together the salt, all the spices and the baking powder and stir into the flour. (Mr Aslam uses no water in his batter!) Add the onions, potatoes and spinach or other vegetables, dig in with your hands and mix together until the flour mixture coats all the vegetables.

Leave to stand for 1 hour. The water from the vegetables will seep into the flour to make a batter that will bind things together.

Stage 3: Shaping and frying the pakoras
Wet your hands. Divide the mixture and squeeze into rough 5 cm / 2 inch balls.

Put enough oil into a saucepan to make 6 cm / 2 1/2 inches depth. Heat it over a fast flame. Lower some of the vegetable balls into the hot oil and deep fry them for 2 minutes. Repeat until they are all cooked.

Drain them on kitchen paper and serve warm with Balti dip (page 145) and Imli sauce (page 146).

Chef Nazu cooks over high heat!

CHICKEN, QUAIL AND DUCK BALTIS

AKASH'S CHICKEN DHANSAK BALTI

(Proprietor M. Abdul Kadir, Chefs M. Abdul and A. Nesar)

Sweet and sour, this Balti has the texture and nutty flavour of lentils contrasting with the smoothness and creamy taste of chicken.

4 Stages • Fairly hot • A good, substantial dinner party Balti • Serves 4

4 large boned chicken breasts, each cut
    into 6 pieces
225 g / 8 oz yellow split peas
6 tbsp vegetable oil
2.5 cm / 1 inch cube fresh ginger, peeled
    and grated
6 garlic cloves, crushed
4 tsp garam masala (page 25)

10 tsp Balti spice mix (page 26)
3-4 tsp chilli powder
4 ladles of Akash's Balti paste
4 rings of canned pineapple, chopped
4-6 tbsp pineapple juice from the can
6 ladles of Balti sauce
fresh coriander leaves to garnish

Stage 1: Making the Balti sauce
See page 24.

Stage 2: Making the Akash Balti paste
See page 107.

Stage 3: Pre-cooking the split peas
See page 24.

Stage 4: Balti method
Put a large wok on a high flame and heat the oil. Fry the ginger and garlic for 3 minutes. Then add, in quick succession and stirring when you can, the garam masala, Balti spice mix, chilli powder, and the Akash Balti paste. Stir well. Put in the cooked split peas, the slices of pineapple and some of the juice to moisten the mixture. Now put in the chicken pieces and the Balti sauce. Shake and stir vigorously. Cook, still stirring, for 5 more minutes, or until the chicken is heated through.

Warm 4 Balti bowls and divide the mixture among them. Garnish with a few coriander leaves and serve.

AL MOUGHAL'S CHICKEN CHOLLEY (CHICK PEA) BALTI

(Proprietor and Chef Mr Moughal)

A good, basic, hearty Balti.

3 Stages • Not too hot • A family meal • Serves 4

*4 boned chicken breasts, each cut into
    6 pieces*
*200 g / 7 oz dried chick peas, or use a
    large can*
6 tbsp vegetable oil
4 tomatoes, chopped

1 tsp garam masala (page 25)
1/2 tsp chilli powder
1 tsp ground coriander
1 tsp garlic powder
1 tbsp chopped fresh coriander

Stage 1: Pre-cooking the chick peas

See page 24. Or open the can and drain well.

Stage 2: Pre-cooking the chicken and making the Balti sauce

See page 22.

Stage 3: Balti method

Heat the oil in a large wok over moderate heat and fry the tomatoes for a few seconds to soften them. Put in the pre-cooked chicken and chick peas. Add the garam masala, chilli powder, ground coriander and garlic powder. Stir-fry for 3 minutes.

Put in the Balti sauce and chopped coriander. Turn the heat to low and stir-fry, gently, for 4 more minutes.

Divide among 4 warmed Balti bowls and serve.

BALTI TOWERS' BALTI MIX
(Proprietor Mr M. Sadique, Chef Mohammed Basharat)

A slightly sweet Balti with the different flavours and textures of lamb, chicken, prawns and mushrooms hinting at their subtle presence in the overall taste.

3 Stages • Mild • A dinner party or special occasion dish • Serves 4

340 g / 3/4 lb boned chicken breasts, cut into cubes
450 g / 1 lb boned lamb, cut into cubes and par-cooked (using ingredients on page 22)
225 g / 8 oz peeled cooked prawns
10 tbsp vegetable ghee or oil
2 x 4 cm / 1 1/2 inch cubes fresh ginger, peeled and grated

12 large garlic cloves, crushed
85 g / 3 oz button mushrooms, sliced
10 ladles of Balti sauce
2 tbsp dried methi
2 tomatoes, quartered
1 1/2 tsp garam masala (page 25)
1 tbsp chopped fresh coriander

Stage 1: Par-cooking the lamb and making the Balti sauce
See page 22, halving the ingredients.

Stage 2: Making the extra Balti sauce
See page 24.

Stage 3: Balti method
Heat the ghee or oil in a large wok over a moderately high flame. Fry the ginger and garlic for half a minute. Add the chicken pieces and stir-fry for 10 minutes. Put in the prawns and stir well. They go in at this early stage, Mr Basharat says, so that they swap their liquid for the flavour of the ginger and garlic and keep their separate identity in the strong company they will be keeping!

Add the mushrooms. Stir-fry for 1 minute and then put in the lamb. Immediately ladle in the Balti sauce and stir the fried mixture into this. Add the methi and quarters of tomato. Turn the heat to low and cook, still stirring, for about 7 minutes or until the chicken is cooked and the meat is heated through.

Divide among 4 warmed Balti bowls and garnish each with a sprinkle of garam masala and a generous pinch of chopped coriander.

BHANGRA BEAT'S HAASH (DUCK) BALTI
(Partners Mr Kabir and Mr Shamim, Chef Mr Sadiqur Choudhury)

Mr Choudhury wrote and published the first ever Balti recipes in 1992. Here he gives a wonderful and unusual dish. The gamey flavour of duck goes so well with the spices.

2 Stages • Medium spiced • A dish for a special occasion • Serves 4

900 g / 2 lb skinned, boned duck, cut into
   3-4 cm / 1¼-1½ inch chunks
8 tbsp vegetable oil
3 onions, chopped, 1 very finely
1 small green pepper, seeded and very
   finely chopped
2.5 cm / 1 inch cube fresh ginger, peeled
   and grated
3 large garlic cloves, crushed
2 tsp turmeric powder
1¼ tsp salt

115 ml / 4 fl oz orange juice
1 fresh green chilli, chopped
1 tbsp chopped fresh coriander
1 tbsp dried methi
½ tsp made English mustard
1 tsp ground coriander
1½ tsp ground cumin
1 tbsp tomato purée
1½ tsp garam masala (page 25)
½ tsp chilli powder

Stage 1: Par-cooking the duck
Heat the oil in a large wok over high heat and fry the very finely chopped onion, the green pepper, ginger and garlic until the onion is starting to change colour. Put in the chunks of duck and sear on all sides. Add the turmeric, salt and 300 ml / ½ pint water. Bring to the boil and cook, stirring frequently, for 15 minutes.

Stage 2: Balti method
Put in all the other ingredients and stir and mix well. Turn the heat down to moderate, cover the wok and cook for 20 more minutes, stirring occasionally to prevent sticking.

Remove the lid, turn the heat to low and simmer for another 20-25 minutes, stirring occasionally and very gently.

Remove from the heat, put the lid back on and let the Balti rest for 10 minutes.

Heat through quickly, then divide among 4 warmed Balti bowls. Serve with naan, chapati (here Mr Choudry is generous to untrained palates), rice or even chips!

BUTTS' (RE-NAMED TABAQ) QUAIL BALTI
(Proprietor Mrs Butt, Chef Mr Nazir)

Balti cuisine has evolved into a Birmingham phenomenon. Quail is one of the enduring links with Pakistan. This recipe makes a superb and different dish. Serve with a vegetable Balti as a side dish.

3 Stages • Medium • A dinner party recipe • Serves 4

4 quails, roughly jointed
7 tbsp vegetable oil
4 onions, finely chopped
2 fresh green chillies, very finely chopped
4 large garlic cloves, crushed
6 brown cardamoms, broken slightly open
6 tomatoes, chopped

4 cm / 1¹/₂ inch cube fresh ginger, peeled and grated
1 tbsp chopped fresh coriander
2 tsp garam masala (page 25)
5 tsp Balti spice mix (page 26)
³/₄ tsp ground ginger
¹/₂ tsp salt

Stage 1: Cooking the quails
Heat 2 tablespoons of oil in a heavy saucepan over moderately high heat. Lower the quail pieces into it and brown them on all sides without attempting to cook them. Take them out, shaking off as much oil as possible and set aside.

In the oil remaining in the pan fry 1 of the chopped onions, stirring until it starts to turn golden. Add the chillies and 1 of the cloves of garlic. Fry for 5 minutes. Add 350 ml / 12 floz water, the quails and 2 of the cardamoms. Bring to the boil. Cover the pan, turn the heat right down and simmer for 20 minutes or until the quails are tender. Stir occasionally during this time. Remove the quails and set them aside again.

Stage 2: Making the Balti sauce
To the remaining liquid in the pan add the rest of the onions, half of the tomatoes, 3 more tablespoons of oil and the rest of the cardamoms. Bring back to the boil and in 7-8 minutes you will have a stiff soup. When this has cooled a little remove the cardamoms and spoon the mixture into a blender or food processor and liquidise it.

Stage 3: Balti method
Heat the remaining oil in a large wok over a high heat. Add the ginger, the rest of the garlic and tomatoes, the chopped coriander, garam masala, Balti spice mix, ginger powder, salt and the quails. Shake and stir vigorously while you do all this. (In Mr Nazir's hands the dish flamed spectacularly!) Cook on high heat for 1¹/₂-2 minutes. If the mixture starts to get dry add a little more Balti sauce.

Divide among 4 warmed Balti bowls and serve with naan bread.

GRAND TANDOORI'S CHICKEN AND BHINDI (LADIES' FINGERS) BALTI

(Proprietor and Chef Mr Asif Butt)

Mr Butt has a rather different way of cooking a Balti. He starts with liquidised onions. The Balti sauce and then the Balti itself are built up in the wok. You could even show off and invite your guests into the kitchen to watch you cook.

1 Stage • Medium hot • Suitable for any Balti occasion • Serves 4

4 small boned chicken breasts, skinned
    and each cut into 6 pieces
450 g / 1 lb ladies' fingers (okra), top-
    and-tailed
10 tbsp vegetable oil
5 onions, chopped and then liquidised
    with a little water
1 or 2 brown cardamoms, broken slightly
    open

4 cm / 1½ inch cinnamon stick
1 tsp turmeric powder
1 tsp paprika
1½ tsp salt
1 tbsp garlic powder
1 tbsp ground ginger
1½ tsp chilli powder
2 tbsp chopped fresh coriander
1 tsp garam masala (page 25)

Heat the oil in a large wok over moderate heat and fry the ladies' fingers until just tender. If they are large slice them in half lengthways. Remove them with a slotted spoon and keep to one side.

Fry the liquidised onions in the oil remaining in the wok until soft and just turning colour. Stir in the cardamoms, cinnamon, turmeric, paprika, salt, and garlic, ginger and chilli powders. Moisten with a little water.

Put in the chopped coriander and the chicken pieces. Bring to the boil and stir-fry for 10 minutes. Put in the ladies' fingers and stir-fry for 8-10 more minutes or until the chicken is cooked (test with a fork).

Divide among 4 warmed Balti bowls and serve sprinkled with garam masala.

I AM THE KING BALTI'S CHICKEN AND MUSHROOM BALTI
(Chef Mr Saeed)

A very popular Balti dish in Birmingham from a very popular Baltihouse. The 'I am the King Balti' interests me for having a drawing by George Grosz, a German expressionist artist, in its logo! In spite, or because, of this reference to decadence the place is always full. This recipe contains what Mr Saeed refers to as 'our secret ingredient - tandoori masala!' You can buy it almost anywhere.

2 Stages • Subtly spiced • Suitable for entertaining • Serves 4

1 x 1.4 kg / 3 lb chicken breast and leg pieces, pre-cooked
10 tbsp vegetable oil
2 fresh green chillies, finely chopped
3 small tomatoes, chopped
5 cm / 2 inch cube fresh ginger, peeled and grated
12 garlic cloves, crushed

1 tsp salt
1¹/₂ tbsp turmeric powder
4 palmfuls of dried methi
115 g / ¹/₄ lb mushrooms, sliced
2 tbsp chopped fresh coriander
1¹/₂ tbsp tandoori masala powder
¹/₂-³/₄ tsp garam masala (page 25)

Stage 1: Pre-cooking the chicken and making the Balti sauce
See page 22.

Stage 2: Balti method
Heat the oil in a large wok over moderately high heat. Fry the the chillies, tomatoes, ginger and garlic for 1 minute. Add the diced chicken, salt and turmeric. Stir-fry for 3 minutes.

Turn the heat down to moderate and add the methi and 6 ladles of the Balti sauce. Stir-fry for 5 minutes. Add the sliced mushrooms and the coriander and cook for 2 more minutes. Stir in the 'secret' ingredient - tandoori masala powder!

Divide among 4 warmed Balti bowls and sprinkle a pinch of garam masala over each to 'aromatise' the dish as you serve it.

ISTAFA'S MURGHI MAKHANI BALTI

(Proprietor Mrs Shabeen Sultana, Chef Mr Moor Ahmed)

This is a chicken tikka dish in a yoghurt, cream and coconut sauce. It's very rich and, in Mr Ahmed's subtle orchestration of ingredients, seasoning and spices, it's an absolute delight. One of the stages is making the very special Istafa Balti sauce. You could save time by using one of our simpler Balti sauce recipes (pages 24–5) but of course the dish won't be true to the restaurant's. (Time could also be saved using commercially prepared chicken tikka.)

3 Stages • Medium • A dinner party recipe • Serves 6

1.4 kg / 3 lb boned chicken pieces, skinned, tandoori marinaded and cooked
FOR THE ISTAFA BALTI SAUCE:
5 bay leaves
10 cm / 4 inch cinnamon stick
4 black cardamoms
4 green cardamoms
1½ tbsp vegetable ghee or oil
4 onions, liquidised with a little water
4 plum tomatoes, peeled fresh or canned, chopped
1 tsp tomato purée
1½ tsp salt
3 cm / 1¼ inch cube fresh ginger, peeled and grated
8 large garlic cloves, crushed
600 ml / 1 pint milk
1½ tbsp pre-cooked yellow split peas (page 24)
1 large carrot, sliced

½ green pepper, seeded and diced
2 tsp paprika
1 tsp turmeric powder
1 tsp ground cumin
1 tsp curry powder
½ tsp garam masala (page 25)
2 tsp ground coriander
FOR THE BALTI STAGE:
6 tbsp vegetable ghee or oil
2 onions, liquidised with a little water
3 cm / 1¼ inch cube fresh ginger, peeled and grated
2 tbsp finely ground unsalted cashew nuts
2 tsp sugar
1½ tbsp dessicated coconut
1½ tbsp coconut cream
1½ tbsp dried methi
2 tbsp single cream
2 tbsp plain yoghurt
150 ml / ¼ pint milk

Stage 1: Making the chicken tikka
See page 20, doubling the marinade ingredients. Or use bought, cooked chicken tikka.

Stage 2: Making the Balti sauce
First make up the spice infusion. In a small pan combine the bay leaves,

cinnamon, both sorts of cardamoms and enough water to cover the spices (about 50 ml / 2 fl oz). Bring to the boil and cook over a moderate heat for 3 minutes. Remove from the heat and let the spices infuse while you continue with the Balti sauce.

Heat the ghee or oil in a large saucepan on moderate heat and fry the liquidised onions until they are starting to change colour. Add the tomatoes, tomato purée, salt, ginger, garlic, milk, split peas, carrot and green pepper. Bring back to the boil, then turn the heat to low and simmer for 15 minutes.

Strain the spiced infusion into the large pan of sauce; discard the whole spices. Add the paprika, turmeric, ground cumin, curry powder, garam masala and ground coriander and stir them all in vigorously. Check that the sauce is not getting too dry, adding a little water if necessary. With the heat on moderate let it boil gently, stirring occasionally, for 20 minutes.

Check the seasoning. Remove the pan from the heat and let it cool. Liquidise the contents of the pan and this is your Istafa Balti sauce.

Stage 3: Balti method

Heat the ghee or oil in a large wok over moderate heat and fry the onions until golden brown. Stir in the ginger and 3 ladles of Balti sauce. Turn the heat down and cook, stirring, for 5 minutes. Put in the cashew nuts, sugar, ground coconut and coconut cream, the chicken tikka and methi. Stir everything well. Still stirring, add the cream and yoghurt. Dribble the milk in gradually. Cook gently for a further 10 minutes, stirring occasionally and adding more Balti sauce if the dish becomes too dry.

Divide among 4 warmed Balti bowls and serve.

KAMRAN'S CHICKEN BALTI WITH JALFREZI

(Proprietors and Chefs Ansar and Malik Farakh)

The fresh peppery quality of spring onions and quite a lot of green pepper make the typical 'jalfrezi' taste. It works here so well with the chicken.

2 Stages • Medium • Suitable for all Balti opportunities • Serves 4

1 x 1.5 kg / 3¹/₄ lb chicken breast and leg
   pieces pre-cooked
8 tbsp vegetable oil
3 large mild onions, chopped
1 green pepper, seeded and diced
3 tomatoes, chopped
3 tbsp chopped spring onions
3 tsp garam masala (page 25)

2 tsp dried methi, rubbed between your
   palms
2 heaped tbsp tomato purée
4 cm / 1¹/₂ inch cube fresh ginger, peeled
   and grated
7 garlic cloves, crushed
1 tbsp chopped fresh coriander

Stage 1: Pre-cooking the chicken and making the Balti sauce

See page 22.

Stage 2: Balti method

Heat the oil in a large wok over moderately high heat and fry the chopped large onions until they are soft and just turning colour. Add the green pepper and tomatoes. Stir-fry, breaking up the tomatoes with the spoon. When they are reduced to a pulp stir in the spring onions, 2 teaspoons of garam masala, the rubbed methi, tomato purée, ginger and garlic. Stir-fry for 5 minutes.

Add the chicken and 5-6 ladles of the Balti sauce. Stir-fry for 2 more minutes. Add 1 teaspoon of the chopped coriander and stir-fry again for another minute. The oil will start to separate; spoon off what you can.

Divide among 4 warmed Balti bowls, garnish with a sprinkle of garam masala and a pinch of chopped coriander, and serve.

KHANUM'S CHICKEN PATHIA BALTI

(Proprietors Diana and Derek, Chef Mr Ali)

It is fascinating how combinations of ingredients can create an unexpected flavour.
In our notes we wrote 'fruity/nutty'. There are no fruit or nuts in this Balti. The peppers,
tomatoes, fresh and puréed, and lemon juice work together to make it sweet and sour, hot
and dry.

2 Stages • Has enough class for a dinner party but is simple enough to cook more often • Serves 4

4 large boned chicken breasts, pre-cooked
7 tbsp vegetable oil
4 cm / 1¹/₂ inch cube fresh ginger, peeled and grated
6 large garlic cloves, crushed
2 onions, chopped
2 fresh green chillies, finely chopped
2 green peppers, seeded and diced
2 tsp dried methi

salt to taste
5 tsp Balti spice mix (page 26)
4 tomatoes, chopped
2 heaped tsp tomato purée
2 tbsp lemon juice
1 tbsp sugar
5-6 ladles of Balti sauce
2 tsp chopped fresh coriander to garnish

Stage 1: Pre-cooking the chicken and making the Balti sauce
See page 22.

Stage 2: Balti method
Heat the oil in a large wok over moderately high heat and stir-fry the ginger and garlic for 1 minute. Put in the onions and fry until they are turning brown. Add the chillies, green peppers, and 3/4 teaspoon of salt. Stir and shake. Add the spice mix, tomatoes, tomato purée, lemon juice, sugar and 5 ladles of Balti sauce.

Stir in the chicken pieces. Add the methi and cook, stirring all the time, for about 4 minutes. The chicken should be thoroughly heated through. Adjust the moisture of the dish by reducing, or by adding more Balti sauce. It is supposed to be fairly dry. Adjust seasoning.

Divide among 4 warmed Balti bowls and serve garnished with fresh coriander.

KHYBER PASS' BALTI CHICKEN TIKKA MASALA
(Chef Mr Shabir)

Chicken tikka masala can be garish owing to liberal amounts of food colouring. This recipe is subtle both in colour and in taste. It is spicy but not too hot.

3 Stages • Medium hot • Suitable for a dinner party • Serves 4

570 g / 1¼ lb chicken tikka
8 tbsp vegetable oil
2 small tomatoes, thickly sliced
1 tbsp garlic powder
2 tsp turmeric powder
1½ tsp tandoori powder or paste
1½ tsp Patak's kashmiri masala (optional)
4 tbsp plain yoghurt
1½ tbsp chopped fresh coriander

2 tsp garam masala (page 25)
1 tbsp dried methi, stalks picked out,
    rubbed between your hands
5 ladles of Balti sauce
2 tbsp plain yoghurt mixed with 1–1½
    tbsp of red food colouring
2.5 cm / 1 inch cube fresh ginger, peeled
    and grated

Stage 1: Making the chicken tikka
See page 20.

Stage 2: Making the Balti sauce
See page 24.

Stage 3: Balti method
Bring the vegetable oil to sizzling hot in a large wok and add the tomatoes and the garlic powder (this, Mr Shabir says, gives the strong pure garlic flavour without the onion-ness of fresh garlic!). Stir them well in. Add the turmeric, tandoori powder or paste, and kashmiri masala if you are using it. Put in the plain yoghurt, a table-spoon at a time, stirring between each to moisten the mixture.

Add the chicken tikka. Stir and shake vigorously, making sure all the pieces of chicken are well coated. Turn the heat up to high and stir in the fresh coriander, garam masala and methi. The heat will sear their flavour into the meat, Mr Shabir explains.

After 1 minute of stirring add the Balti sauce, ginger and the coloured yoghurt. Stir these well in too and simmer for about 5 minutes. All the ingredients should look well integrated, and what little oil is still visible should be separating around the edges.

Give a final stir, then divide among 4 warmed Balti bowls and serve.

MOKHAM'S BALTI EXOTICA WITH PASTA
(Proprietors 'Naz' and 'Kal', Chef 'Mr Q' Qayoum)

Yes, pasta! Real Italian pasta! Mr Q is a very innovative chef. This isn't as complicated as it looks. It uses a special tomato Balti sauce instead of an orthodox one, but it doesn't take long to make.

4 Stages • Medium spiced • A dinner party dish with built-in 'topic of conversation'! • Serves 4–6

450 g / 1 lb boned lamb, cubed and par-cooked (using ingredients from page 22)
450 g / 1 lb boned chicken breasts, cut into chunks
115 g / 4 oz pasta shells or macaroni
1 bouquet garni (page 26)
400 g / 14 oz tomatoes, peeled, or use canned, plus 4 tomatoes, chopped
115 g / 4 oz butter
1¹/₂ tbsp sugar
2 tsp salt
2 tsp chilli powder
7 tsp garam masala (page 25)
5 tsp dried methi

3¹/₂ tsp ground cumin
3¹/₂ tsp ground coriander
8 tbsp vegetable oil
3 onions, thinly sliced
1 green pepper, seeded and diced
2 cm / ³/₄ inch cube fresh ginger, peeled and grated
5 garlic cloves, crushed
5 tsp Balti spice mix (page 26)
85 g / 3 oz button mushrooms, sliced
225 g / ¹/₂ lb peeled cooked prawns
1 tsp turmeric powder
2 tsp paprika
1 tbsp chopped fresh coriander

Stage 1: Par-cooking the lamb and making the Balti sauce
See page 22, halving the ingredients.

Stage 2: Pre-cooking the pasta
Cook the pasta in a large pan of boiling salted water for 5 minutes. Drain well. Rinse with hot water and set aside.

Stage 3: Making the tomato Balti sauce
Put the peeled tomatoes in a medium saucepan, with a little water if you are using fresh ones, and heat. Into this melt the butter and stir in the sugar, 1 teaspoon each of salt and chilli powder, 5 teaspoons of garam masala, 3 teaspoons of methi and 2¹/₂ teaspoons each of ground cumin and coriander. Cook, gently stirring, for 3-4 minutes. Remove from the heat and allow to cool, then liquidise in a blender or food processor.

Stage 4: Balti method

Put your largest wok on the stove with the heat turned up high and pour in the oil (you need a lot, but when the dish is finished you can spoon off the excess). When it is hot add the onion slices, green pepper, chopped tomatoes, and all but 1/2 teaspoon each of the ginger and garlic. Stir in the rest of the salt and chilli powder and the chicken breasts. Turn the heat to low and, stirring all the time, cook until the onions are soft. Add the spice mix and cook for another minute.

Now stir in the Balti tomato sauce. The mixture might be quite thick. If it is add a little water. Stir well and add the rest of the garam masala, methi and ground cumin and coriander. Cover the wok and simmer for 8 minutes.

Take the lid off, stir the contents of the wok and add the mushrooms and the rest of the ginger and garlic. Now put in the par-cooked meat. After 2 minutes of stirring put in the prawns. If the mixture is too dry add some more water, taking care always to keep the dish on the dry side.

Add the pasta and again more water if necessary. Cook, stirring often, for a further 15 minutes. The comparatively long cooking time makes for an integrated spice taste.

Divide among 4 warmed Balti bowls. Serve garnished with a generous pinch of chopped coriander.

NIRALA'S CHICKEN AND BLACK EYE BEAN BALTI

(Proprietor Mr Aslam, Chef Mr Asif)

The secret is in the garam masala, Mr Asif says. The proprietor's mother grinds this at home and not even the chef knows what goes into it. In deference to her we grind ours specially and include black cumin seeds and a little ajwan (lovage seed).

4 Stages • Medium • A dinner party recipe • Serves 4

4 large boned chicken breasts, each cut into 6 pieces
400 g / 14 oz dried black eye beans, or use canned beans
1 tsp salt
2 tsp turmeric powder
1 tsp chilli powder
4 cm / 1½ inch cube fresh ginger, peeled and grated

6 garlic cloves, crushed
2 tsp garam masala (page 25)
1 tsp black cumin seed, ground
½ tsp lovage seeds (ajwan), ground
6 tbsp vegetable oil
6-7 ladles of Balti sauce
1½ tbsp dried methi
1 tbsp chopped fresh coriander

Stage 1: Pre-cooking the black eye beans and chicken

Put the beans into a pan with water to cover. Add the salt, 1 teaspoon turmeric, the chilli powder, and 1 teaspoon each of the grated ginger and crushed garlic and bring to the boil. Simmer for 5 minutes. Remove from the heat and let the beans soak for 1 hour. Bring back to the boil, then cover and simmer for 15 minutes.

Put in the pieces of chicken and simmer gently for a further 20 minutes. Check that both the beans and the chicken are tender. Remove the chicken, drain the beans and keep ready for the Balti.

Stage 2: Making the Balti sauce

See page 24.

Stage 3: Making the garam masala

Freshly grind the garam masala (see page 25), adding the ground black cumin and lovage seeds to the other spices.

Stage 4: Balti method

Heat the oil in a large wok over moderately high heat and fry the rest of the ginger and garlic for 30 seconds. Ladle in the Balti sauce, and add the methi, the remaining turmeric, fresh coriander and garam masala. Stir well and cook for 1 minute. Put in the chicken and the beans and stir-cook for 7-8 minutes.

Warm 4 Balti bowls and divide the mixture. Serve with naan bread.

PARIS'S BALTI CHICKEN MALAYA
(Proprietor Raj Mhoom, Chef Mr Mih)

'Malaya' always means with fruit, in Baltihouses at least, and fruit almost always means pineapple. But try this also with mango pieces, making up the same quantity as the pineapple. The sugariness of the fruit counteracts the different sort of sweetness that tomatoes and onions have, and the complexity of the aroma of Balti spice mix and the other spices combine to make a delicious dish. It's only a 1-stage recipe, but quite a long one – about 20-25 minutes. This may make it a supper party dish rather than for the family, but they'd love it too.

1 Stage • Mildly spiced • Serves 4

4 chicken breasts, boned and diced
225 g / 1/2 lb onions, chopped
2 tsp salt
3 cm / 11/4 inch cube fresh ginger, peeled and grated
2 large garlic cloves, crushed
1 tsp turmeric powder
2 tsp dried methi
115 g / 4 oz unsalted butter or 8 tbsp vegetable oil
2 tsp Balti spice mix (page 26)

1/2 tsp curry powder
4 whole cloves
1 black, or 4 green, cardamoms, broken slightly open
4 cm / 11/2 inch cinnamon stick
2 black peppercorns
1 tomato, chopped
2 tbsp chopped fresh coriander
juice of 1/2 lemon
2 rings of canned pineapple, chopped
2 tsp pineapple juice from the can

With your wok on a lowish heat bring 150 ml / 1/4 pint water to the boil with the chicken, onions, salt, ginger, garlic, turmeric and the dried methi. Cover with a lid and simmer for 20 minutes or until the chicken is tender.

Add the butter or oil, the Balti spice mix, curry powder, cloves, cardamoms, cinnamon stick and peppercorns and stir them in. Cook gently for 5 minutes. Put in the tomato, fresh coriander, lemon juice, and pineapple chunks and juice. Add up to another 150 ml / 1/4 pint water (the dish should not be too wet). Simmer for 5 minutes.

Divide among 4 warmed Balti bowls and serve.

PARIS'S CHICKEN, AUBERGINE AND GREEN PEPPER BALTI

(Proprietor Mr Armzan, Partner Farid (John), Chef M Nazir)

Aubergine has a rather meaty taste and works well here with the chicken and green pepper. You could use the basic recipe and choose any fried vegetables.

2 Stages • Medium • A very good family Balti • Serves 4

680 g / 1¹/₂ lb boned chicken, pre-cooked
1 large aubergine, cut into large dice
1 green pepper, seeded and diced
8 tbsp vegetable oil
1 fresh green chilli, finely chopped
5 tsp Balti spice mix (page 26)

6 large garlic cloves, crushed
2 tomatoes, roughly chopped
1¹/₂ tsp dried methi
6 ladles of Balti sauce
1 tsp garam masala (page 25)
1 tbsp chopped fresh coriander to garnish

Stage 1: Pre-cooking the chicken and making the Balti sauce

See page 22.

Stage 2: Balti method

Heat half of the oil in a large wok over moderate heat. When it is hot fry the aubergine pieces with the chopped green chilli and Balti spice mix until the aubergine is just tender. Remove the pieces with a slotted spoon, leaving behind as much of the spiced oil as possible, and keep them to one side.

Add the rest of the oil to the wok and when hot fry the garlic, tomatoes and green pepper, stirring and breaking up the tomatoes. Add the pieces of chicken, the methi and Balti sauce. Cook, stirring all the time, for 3 minutes. Add the cooked aubergine and cook for another 3 minutes.

Divide into 4 warmed Balti bowls and sprinkle each with a pinch of garam masala. Garnish with chopped coriander and serve.

PUNJAB PARADISE'S BALTI CHICKEN AND PRAWN

(Proprietor Mr Shabaz, Chef Pinnu Khan, Head waiter Tanveer Choudhry – nickname 'Tan', second name Doori! ha-ha! – who told us this recipe)

Our very first Balti recipe! At the bottom of our stained notebook page, written after we'd cooked our first Balti we've written 'Good! It really does taste authentic'. It's suitable any time you fancy a Balti, and is very easy to cook.

1 Stage • Medium hot • Serves 4

1 x 1.5 kg / 3¼ lb chicken breast and leg pieces, skinned
225 g / ½ lb small peeled cooked prawns
4 tbsp vegetable oil
3 onions, chopped
3 small tomatoes, chopped
4 cm / 1½ inch cube fresh ginger, peeled and grated

5 garlic cloves, crushed
2 fresh green chillies, seeded and finely chopped
1½ tsp salt
170 g / 6 oz button mushrooms, sliced
1 tsp garam masala (page 25)

Heat the oil in a large wok over a high heat. Fry the onions until they are translucent. Add the tomatoes, ginger and garlic. Stir and break up the tomatoes with the spoon as they cook. After 5 minutes add the chillies, salt and 300 ml / ½ pint water. Put in the chicken pieces and bring back to the boil. Stir well. Turn the heat down, cover with a lid and simmer for 25-30 minutes, or until the chicken is tender.

Remove the pieces of chicken with a slotted spoon and allow to cool. Turn the heat up and reduce the sauce left in the wok until it is the consistency of thick soup.

When it is cool enough to handle remove the chicken meat from the bones and cut into chunks. Add to the wok. Add the prawns and cook on medium heat for 5 minutes. Stir in the mushrooms and stir-fry for 5 more minutes.

Sprinkle with garam masala before you divide among 4 warmed Balti bowls. Serve with garlic naan.

RICE AND SPICE'S BALTI MOGLAI CHICKEN
(Proprietor Mr Meenar Islam, Chef Mr Shofique Miah)

Rice and Spice was London's first Baltihouse. This is a very rich dish with a sweetish sauce of cream and almonds.

1 Stage • Very mild • Suitable for a dinner party • Serves 4

1 large chicken, skinned, meat removed
    and cut into chunks
370 g / 13 oz butter ghee or unsalted
    butter
2 onions, grated
2 tsp salt
3 cm / 1¼ inch cube fresh ginger, peeled
    and grated
8 garlic cloves, crushed

6 green cardamoms, broken slightly open
2 x 4 cm / 1½ inch cinnamon sticks
3–4 bay leaves
4 eggs, lightly beaten
4 tbsp sugar
6 tbsp ground almonds
800 ml / 27 fl oz single cream
flaked almonds to garnish

Heat the ghee or butter in a large wok over moderate heat and fry the onions with the salt until translucent. Add the ginger, garlic, cardamoms, cinnamon sticks and bay leaves. Stir-fry until the onions are golden brown.

Add the chunks of chicken and cook, stirring occasionally, for about 13 minutes.

In a small bowl, mix together the eggs, sugar, ground almonds and cream.

Turn the heat right down and pour the egg and cream mixture into the wok. Simmer gently for 5–7 minutes or until the chicken is cooked and tender. Be careful not to overcook the sauce or the eggs and cream will curdle.

Divide among 4 warmed Balti bowls and serve garnished with flaked almonds.

ROYAL NAIM'S CHICKEN MASALA BALTI

(Proprietor Mr Azim, Chef Mohammad Nazir)

A simple chicken Balti with a spicy, yoghurty sauce.

2 Stages • Medium hot • Suitable for a dinner party • Serves 4

4 large boned chicken breasts, each cut
    into 6 pieces
3 tbsp vegetable ghee or oil
2 onions, chopped
2 tomatoes, chopped
2 fresh green chillies, finely chopped
1 tsp turmeric powder
1 tsp ground cumin
1 tsp ground coriander

1 tsp salt
4 cm / 1½ inch cube fresh ginger, peeled
    and grated
6 large garlic cloves, crushed
2 palmfuls of chopped fresh coriander
3-4 ladles of Balti sauce
2 tsp garam masala (page 25)
2 tsp dried methi
300 ml / ½ pint plain yoghurt

Stage 1: Making the Balti sauce
See page 24.

Stage 2: Balti method
Heat the ghee or oil in a large wok over
moderately high heat and fry the onions
until tender. Add the tomatoes and fry
them until they become a pulp, breaking
them up with the spoon. Put in 1 tablespoon of water and add the chillies,
turmeric, cumin, ground coriander and
salt. Stir well and put in the ginger, garlic,

chopped coriander and the chicken. Shake
and stir for 10 minutes.

Add 3 ladles of Balti sauce, the garam
masala and methi. Put the yoghurt in, a
tablespoon at a time, stirring between
each addition. Reduce the heat and
simmer for 8-10 minutes or until the
chicken is tender. Add another ladle of
Balti sauce if you like your Balti with lots
of sauce.

Divide among 4 warmed Balti bowls
and serve.

SALMA'S SPECIAL BALTI
(Proprietors Mr Ali and Mr Aslam, who is also Chef)

One of Mr Aslam's favourite expressions is 'There's a Balti and there's a Balti...Now, this is a Balti!' he says, 'The chef's special!' It makes its own Balti sauce in the cooking and employs what Mr Aslam calls the absolute secret 'red masala'! This turns out to be the bonus of Tandoori cooking, the little bits of highly spiced meat and marinade that are left behind. Here he shows how you can get the same effect at home.

3 Stages • Medium hot, subtly spiced • Serves 4-6

4 boned chicken breasts, each chopped
   into 8 pieces
200 g / 7 oz dried black eye beans, or use
   canned
7 tbsp vegetable oil
3 onions, chopped
4 small tomatoes, roughly chopped
3 tbsp chopped fresh coriander
5 tsp Balti spice mix (page 26)
1 tbsp turmeric powder
1/4 chicken stock cube, crumbled
2 tsp tandoori masala powder
2.5 cm / 1 inch cube fresh ginger, peeled
   and grated
4 garlic cloves, crushed

1 green pepper, seeded and thinly sliced
   lengthwise
150 ml / 1/4 pint plain yoghurt
1 tsp salt
1 tsp chilli powder
1 tsp paprika
2 tsp garam masala, plus a little extra to
   garnish (page 25)
170 g / 6 oz small peeled cooked prawns
400 g / 14 oz canned tinda, drained,
   or pre-cooked turnips, diced
400 g / 14 oz fresh ladies' fingers (okra),
   top-and-tailed and chopped into 4 cm /
   1 1/2 inch lengths, or use canned

Stage 1: Pre-cooking the black eye beans
See page 24. Or open the can and drain well.

Stage 2: Pre-cooking the chicken and making the Balti sauce
Heat 3 tablespoons of the oil in a saucepan and fry the onions over a high heat until they are translucent but haven't changed colour. Turn the heat down to medium-low and stir in 2 of the chopped tomatoes, breaking them up with the side of the spoon as they start to cook. Add 2 tablespoons of the chopped coriander, the Balti spice mix and turmeric. Stir in well, then remove the pan from the heat.

When cool liquidise the contents.

Return the puréed mixture to the pan and add 250 ml / 9 fl oz water. Bring to the boil and add the chicken pieces. Stir well and cook gently for 15 minutes.

Meanwhile, make the alternative 'red masala', if you don't have any bits left from tandoori chicken: Crush together the crumbled stock cube and tandoori masala powder using the back of a spoon.

Stage 3: Balti method

Heat the rest of the oil over a low flame in a large wok and put in the ginger and garlic. Stir for about 1 minute, then add the remaining tomatoes and the green pepper. Allow the tomatoes to break up and the peppers to have some of their crispness taken off, about 3 minutes, then stir in the yoghurt.

Add about two-thirds of the salt (keep the rest for adjusting the flavour later). Now put in the chilli powder, paprika and garam masala. Stir in the remaining chopped coriander. Add the chicken, with its Balti sauce, and the prawns. Add the tinda, or turnips, the ladies' fingers and black eye beans. Add the 'red masala' and stir it in well. Cook gently, without stirring, for 5 minutes.

Stir everything and check to see if you need to add any more salt. Divide among 4 warmed Balti bowls. Sprinkle each with a pinch of garam masala and serve.

SHABAB'S BATTARA (QUAIL) ROGAN JOSH BALTI

(Proprietors the Hussain family, Chef Matloob Hussain)

A fairly exotic dinner party dish, this is designed to tickle the palate rather than fill you to capacity. We've allowed one quail each. If you really want to go to town allow two per Balti.

1 Stage • Mild • Dinner party dish • Serves 4

4 quails, cut in half lengthways
8 tbsp vegetable oil
4 cm / 1½ inch cube fresh ginger, peeled and grated
8 garlic cloves, crushed
4 small tomatoes, chopped
2 onions, chopped
1 green pepper, seeded and chopped

1 tbsp turmeric powder
4 tsp paprika
½ tsp chilli powder
2 tsp salt
3 tbsp chopped fresh coriander
½ tsp garam masala, plus a little extra to garnish (page 25)
1 tsp dried methi

Heat the oil in a large wok over moderate heat. Fry the ginger, garlic and tomatoes for 2 minutes. Add the onions and green pepper and cook, stirring occasionally, until the onions are just starting to turn brown. Add the turmeric, paprika, chilli powder and salt. Turn the heat right up and stir them all well in. The spices will dry the mixture quite a lot so you might have to add a little water, but no more than about 1 tablespoon at this time.

Put in the quails, the fresh coriander, garam masala and methi. Cook for 5 minutes on moderate heat, stirring all the time. Then add 4 tablespoons of water. Turn the heat to low, cover the wok and simmer gently for 2 more minutes. (If you are using 2 quails per serving, add another 5 minutes to the cooking time.)

Check the seasoning, and if there is too much oil spoon some off. If there is too much sauce turn the heat up and boil uncovered until it has reduced.

Divide among 4 warmed Balti dishes and sprinkle each with a pinch of garam masala. And, as Mr Hussain says, 'Voila!'

Eat with chapatis.

SPICE VALLEY'S TANDOORI STEAM CHICKEN BALTI

(Proprietor Mr Alom, Chef Mr Nazir Ahmed)

This tandoori chicken is about as far from shop-bought as it's possible to be and well worth the investment of time. Mr Ahmed's method is quite complex. It involves cooking chicken in three separate ways, but we've simplified the process slightly, whilst still managing to preserve the moistness of the chicken and without losing the delicious flavour of the marinade.

4 Stages • Spicy • An impressive dinner party Balti • Serves 4

4 chicken legs and 4 chicken breasts, on the bone, skinned
1/2 tbsp vinegar

FOR THE MARINADE:
2 tsp garam masala (page 25)
1 tbsp curry powder
1/2 tsp chilli powder
1 tsp salt
11/2 tbsp ground coriander
11/2 tbsp dried methi
1 tbsp tandoori masala paste
11/2 tbsp concentrated mint sauce
300 ml / 1/2 pint plain yoghurt
juice of 2 lemons
1-11/2 tbsp red food colouring (optional)
1 tbsp vegetable oil

FOR THE BALTI STAGE:
8 tbsp vegetable ghee
12 large garlic cloves, crushed
1/2 green pepper, seeded and chopped
2 small fresh green chillies, finely chopped
3 onions, chopped
1 tsp salt
1 tsp curry powder
2 tbsp dried methi
4 tbsp chopped fresh coriander
2 tsp garam masala (page 25)
11/2 tbsp tomato purée
5 tomatoes, chopped
11/2 tbsp cumin seeds
4-6 ladles of Balti sauce
2 tbsp Patak's kashmiri masala, or use 8 garlic cloves, crushed, and 1 tbsp lime pickle

Stage 1: Marinading the chicken
(You can do this the day before.) Make deep slashing cuts in the chicken pieces, right to the bone, keeping the overall shape of each joint. Rinse the pieces of chicken in a bowl of cold water to which the vinegar has been added. Pat dry with kitchen paper.

To make the marinade, put all the ingredients into a large mixing bowl and mix to a runny paste.

Put the chicken pieces into the

marinade and work and squeeze the paste thoroughly into the slits. Cover with cling film and leave in a cool place for 3 or 4 hours; overnight would be even better. (Mr Ahmed only allowed 20 minutes for his marinade and it worked very well, but he says the longer the better!)

Stage 2: Tandoori cooking the chicken

See page 20; it is important that the chicken is only just cooked. You can remove the meat from the bones or leave it on in this Balti. Reserve the left-over marinade.

Stage 3: Making the Balti sauce

See page 24.

Stage 4: Balti method

Over a high flame heat the ghee in a large wok and fry the garlic, green pepper, chillies and onions until starting to soften. Stir and shake with the Balti rhythm. Add the salt, curry powder, methi, chopped coriander, garam masala and tomato purée. Stir them well in and moisten with the chopped tomatoes. Add the cumin seeds. Ladle the Balti sauce over everything and spoon in the kashmiri masala.

Now put in the pieces of chicken and the remains of the marinade, stirring them well in. Turn the heat to a moderate flame and cook, stirring occasionally, for 10 minutes.

Heat 4 Balti bowls until they are really hot. Place them on heatproof mats. Divide the mixture in the wok among the hot bowls. It should sizzle as you do it. Cover the bowls immediately and take them quickly to the table.

Remove the lids and release an aromatic steam that will get everyone's mouth watering. No garnish is needed.

Markhams' Special Balti stove.

MEAT BALTIS

ADIL'S TINDA GOSHT (LAMB) BALTI
(Manager and Chef Mr Ashiraf)

Tinda is a vegetable typical of the Punjab. It has a very specific taste and is almost impossible to get outside Asian stores. Turnips will give a different but delicious dish.

2 Stages • Exceptionally mild • A family dish • Serves 4

FOR THE PAR-COOKING STAGE:
680 g / 1 1/2 lb boned leg of lamb, cut into
*   2 cm / 3/4 inch cubes*
3 onions, chopped
4 tomatoes, chopped
2 cm / 3/4 inch cube fresh ginger, peeled
*   and grated*
5 garlic cloves, crushed
1/2 fresh green chilli, finely chopped
3/4 tsp salt
FOR THE BALTI STAGE:
400 g / 14 oz canned tinda, drained and
quartered, or 3 small turnips, peeled
*   and chopped into 1 cm / 1/2 inch dice*
8 tbsp vegetable oil
2 tsp ground coriander
2 tsp ground cumin
2 tsp turmeric powder
8 black peppercorns
3 x 4 cm / 1 1/2 inch cinnamon sticks
3 black cardamoms, broken slightly open
6 whole cloves
2 tsp chopped fresh coriander

Stage 1: Par-cooking the meat and making the Balti sauce

Put the onions and tomatoes into a large saucepan with 250 ml / 9 fl oz water. Bring nearly to the boil. Add the meat, ginger, garlic, chopped chilli and salt. Add a little more water if the mixture is too dry. Return to the boil and cook gently with the lid on for 35-40 minutes or until the meat is just barely cooked. Remove the meat with a slotted spoon and keep it warm. Liquidise the remaining liquid. This is your Balti sauce.

Stage 2: Balti method

Use a large wok. Heat the oil on moderate heat and carefully (in case it spits) add 4 ladles of the Balti sauce. In quick succession, stirring as you do it, add the ground coriander, 1 teaspoon of ground cumin, the turmeric, peppercorns, cinnamon, cardamoms and cloves. Make sure all the spices are well mixed in.

Stir in the meat. Turn the heat down, cover with a lid and simmer for 10 minutes. Stir occasionally, adding a little more of the water if you need to.

Add the drained tinda, or the turnips. Simmer, stirring gently, for 10-12 minutes more or until the tinda and the meat are tender. Turnips will need longer to cook.

Remove from the heat, take the cinnamon sticks and cardamoms out, and divide among 4 warmed Balti dishes. Sprinkle each with a pinch of ground cumin, some chopped coriander, and serve.

ALAM GEER'S KEEMA (MINCED LAMB) AND PRAWN BALTI

(Proprietor and Chef Mr Arif)

Prawns are not to be bullied. In the boldest company they hold their own. They work well with the minced lamb and spices in this Balti, quietly insisting their presence.

1 Stage • Medium spiced • Serves 4

680 g / 1¹/₂ lb minced lamb
225 g / ¹/₂ lb peeled cooked prawns
150 ml / ¹/₄ pint vegetable oil
4 large onions, chopped
2 tsp salt
6 whole cloves
2 brown cardamoms, broken slightly open
2 x 1 cm / ¹/₂ inch pieces of cinnamon stick
4 cm / 1¹/₂ inch cube fresh ginger, peeled and grated
4 large garlic cloves, crushed
1 tbsp tomato purée
2 tsp turmeric powder
1 tsp curry powder

1 tsp paprika
1 tsp ground cumin
1 tsp ground coriander
1 tsp garlic powder
1 fresh green chilli, chopped
2 tomatoes, chopped
2 tbsp dried methi
¹/₂ green pepper, seeded and cut into 5 mm / ¹/₄ inch strips
4 large button mushrooms, thinly sliced
palmful of chopped fresh coriander
pinch of garam masala
pinch of chopped fresh coriander
lemon juice

Heat the oil in a large wok on moderate heat. Put in the onions and salt. Stir and turn the heat to low. Cook for 10-15 minutes. Turn up the heat, add 3 tablespoons of water and, in quick succession, drop in the cloves, cardamoms and cinnamon. Stir in the ginger, garlic and the tomato purée. Next add the dry spices – the turmeric, curry powder, paprika, ground cumin, ground coriander and garlic powder. Stir them in well and add the green chilli.

Moisten the mixture with a ladle of water, and put in the chopped tomatoes and the methi. Add the minced lamb and turn until all of it is brown, breaking it up

with the spoon. Add the green pepper. Cover, turn the heat to low and cook gently for 10 minutes, stirring now and then. If the mixture starts to get a little dry add some more water (a tablespoon at a time).

Add the mushrooms and prawns and stir them in gently. Sprinkle the chopped coriander and garam masala over the top. Cover again and continue cooking on a low heat for 3 more minutes. The oil conveniently separates to show you when the dish is ready!

Divide among 4 warmed Balti bowls. Sprinkle each Balti with fresh coriander and lemon juice and serve.

BALTI BAZAAR'S LAMB KESRI (LAMB WITH CABBAGE) BALTI

(Partners Mohammed Abdul Kadir and Rokib Ali who is also Chef)

Mr Ali's garam masala contains 30 ingredients, and it's his secret! We use a good basic garam masala recipe and add a couple of extra spices. The down to earth ingredients make a subtle, spicy Balti.

2 Stages • Mild-medium • A dish for entertaining • Serves 4

900 g / 2 lb boned lamb, cut into 2.5 cm / 1 inch cubes and par-cooked (using ingredients on page 22)
340 g / ¾ lb white cabbage, chopped
8 tbsp vegetable oil
½ tsp turmeric powder
2 tsp freshly ground black pepper
2 onions, chopped
12 garlic cloves, crushed
5 tsp Balti spice mix (page 26)

1 tbsp garam masala (page 25)
2.5 cm / 1 inch cinnamon stick
2 brown cardamoms, broken slightly open
6 whole cloves
½ tsp ground fennel
2 tsp dried methi
½ tsp lovage seed (ajwan), optional
2 tsp salt
6 ladles of Balti sauce
chopped fresh coriander to garnish

Stage 1: Par-cooking the lamb and making the Balti sauce
See page 22.

Stage 2: Cooking the cabbage and the Balti method
Heat 5 tablespoons of the oil in a large wok over moderately high heat. Put the chopped cabbage in and stir-fry for 1 minute. Add the turmeric and 1 teaspoon of the black pepper. Turn the heat to low and cook, stirring occasionally, for 5 minutes or until the cabbage is just tender. Remove the cabbage with a slotted spoon and set aside.

Put in the remaining oil, turn up the heat and fry the onions until translucent. Stir in the other teaspoon of black pepper, the garlic, spice mix, garam masala, cinnamon, cardamoms, whole cloves, fennel, methi, lovage and salt. Add the cooked cabbage and 5 ladles of the Balti sauce and mix well. Bring back to the boil.

Put in the lamb. Cook and stir for 5 minutes. If the mixture is getting too dry add more Balti sauce.

Divide among 4 warmed Balti bowls and serve garnished with fresh coriander.

BRICK LANE'S SONAR BANGLA'S LAMB PASANDA BALTI

(Proprietors Mr Sahid and Emdadul Hoque, Chef Mr T. Miah)

A rich, creamy, sparsely spiced Balti that uses marinaded lamb, which is then grilled and added to the thick almondy Balti sauce at the end of cooking.

4 Stages • Mild • A family Balti • Serves 4

680 g / 1¹/2 lb boned lamb, cut into 4 cm /
*   1¹/2 inch chunks*
FOR THE MARINADE:
2.5 cm / 1 inch cube fresh ginger, peeled
*   and grated*
1 heaped tbsp dried methi
2 tbsp chopped fresh coriander
¹/2 tsp lovage seeds (ajwan), optional
300 ml / ¹/2 pint plain yoghurt
FOR THE BALTI STAGE:
85 g / 3 oz unsalted butter or ghee
8 garlic cloves, crushed

2 onions, chopped
1 tbsp chopped green pepper
1¹/2 tsp salt
6-8 ladles of Balti sauce
4 tbsp desiccated coconut
4 tbsp ground almonds
5 tsp Balti spice mix (page 26)
1 tbsp tomato purée
1 tbsp sugar
1 tbsp sultanas
1¹/2 tbsp flaked almonds
225 ml / 8 fl oz single cream

Stage 1: Making the Balti sauce
See page 24.

Stage 2: Marinading the lamb
Mix the ginger, methi, chopped coriander and lovage seeds into the yoghurt. Put in the lamb and cover thoroughly with marinade. Cover with cling film and chill for a minimum of 2 hours – longer is better.

Stage 3: Grilling the lamb
Preheat the grill on high for 3 minutes. Wipe most of the marinade off the lamb. Thread the chunks on to skewers and grill for about 7 minutes on each side. The meat should still be slightly pink in the middle. Keep warm for the Balti.

Stage 4: Balti method
Heat the butter or ghee in a large wok over moderate heat and fry the garlic until it starts to turn brown. Put in the onions and green pepper and fry until the onions are translucent. Add the salt and 2 ladles of Balti sauce. In quick succession add the rest of the ingredients except the cream. Stir well and add another 4 ladles of Balti sauce. Turn the heat to high and stir-fry for 10 minutes.

Take the chunks of lamb off the skewers and put them into the wok. Cook for 7 more minutes or until the meat is cooked. Add more Balti sauce if necessary and three-quarters of the cream.

Divide among 4 warmed Balti bowls and garnish with a dribble of cream.

DIWAN'S BALTI LAMB BUTTER MASALA
(Proprietor Mr Uddin)

A wonderful, very rich Balti. Definitely not for the calorie conscious, containing as it does butter, cream and almonds. Don't invite any fashion models!

2 Stages • Mild with a touch of sweetness • A luxury dinner party recipe • Serves 4

900 g / 2 lb boned lamb, cut into 4 cm /
   1¹/2 inch cubes, tandoori marinaded
   and cooked
150 g / 5¹/2 oz unsalted butter
4 onions, chopped
4 cm / 1¹/2 inch cube fresh ginger, peeled
   and grated
8 garlic cloves, crushed
1 tbsp ground white pepper

2 tsp ground cumin
2 tsp ground coriander
2 tsp curry powder
8 tomatoes, peeled and chopped, or use
   canned
150 ml / ¹/4 pint plain yoghurt
3 tbsp ground almonds
150 ml / ¹/4 pint double cream
2 tsp dried methi

Stage 1: Making the tandoori lamb
See page 20.

Stage 2: Balti method
Melt the butter in a large wok over moderate heat. When hot, fry the onions, ginger and garlic until the onions are soft. Stir in the white pepper, ground cumin and coriander, curry powder and tomatoes. Put the yoghurt in, 1 tablespoon at a time, stirring each spoonful until it is incorporated. Stir-fry on moderate heat for 5 minutes. If necessary, add a little water to moisten the mixture.

Put in the almonds, cream, methi and the lamb. Turn the heat to low and simmer gently for 10 minutes or until the meat is cooked all the way through.

Divide among 4 warmed Balti bowls and serve.

THE EMPIRE'S ACHARIE MEAT BALTI
(Proprietors Fahim Akhtar and Aslam Perviaz who is also Chef)

Mr Perviaz loves to keep his dishes simple and subtle. 'Acharie' means pickle and this dish has a gentle sour and salty hint of it. There is little sauce. A Balti proud to stand on its own. When asked about quantities for one Mr Perviaz asked 'Is he hungry?'

2 Stages • Medium • Suitable for a dinner party • Serves 4

450 g / 1 lb boned lamb, cut into 3 cm / 1¼ inch pieces
225 g / ½ lb onions, chopped
½ tsp salt
4 cm / 1½ inch cube fresh ginger, peeled and grated
8 large garlic cloves, crushed
1 fresh green chilli, finely chopped
¼ tsp turmeric powder
½ tbsp tomato purée
11 tbsp vegetable oil
1 tsp garam masala (page 25)
3 tbsp chopped fresh coriander, plus 2 palmfuls for later
2 tbsp sauce from lime pickle

Stage 1: Par-cooking the lamb

Put the lamb in a saucepan with the onions, salt and 150 ml / ¼ pint of water. Bring to the boil. Turn the heat to low, cover and simmer for 30 minutes, stirring occasionally to prevent sticking.

While the lamb is cooking assemble the grated ginger, crushed garlic, chilli, turmeric and tomato purée in a blender and liquidise them.

Check to see if the meat is nearly cooked; it should still be pink in the middle. Then stir in 3 tablespoons of the oil and the contents of the blender. Cook on moderate heat, stirring occasionally, for 4 minutes. Add the garam masala and 3 tablespoons fresh coriander and cook for

2 more minutes. Remove from the stove and allow to cool.

Stage 2: Balti method

Heat the rest of the oil in a large wok over a moderately low flame. Add the sauce from lime pickle (you don't want any of the solid lime itself) and fry this in the oil for 1 minute. Add the lamb with 6 tablespoons of its liquid from the saucepan. Stir-fry this for 1 minute. Add 2 palmfuls of chopped coriander and stir-fry another minute.

Remove the meat from the sauce for the dry dish Mr Perviaz prefers, or serve with the sauce, in 4 warmed Balti bowls.

FAISAL SUNDOWN'S KEEMA SAG (MINCED LAMB AND SPINACH) BALTI

(Proprietor and Chef Mr Affar)

A dark, delicious classic Balti dish.

2 Stages • Mild-medium • Suitable for a family meal • Serves 4

680 g / 1½ lb minced lamb
680 g / 1½ lb fresh spinach, chopped
4 tbsp vegetable oil
2 onions, finely chopped
1 tsp garam masala (page 25)
1½ tbsp chopped fresh coriander
½ tsp chilli powder
1 tsp salt

2 tsp dried methi
6 garlic cloves, crushed
50 g / 1¾ oz butter
5 tsp Balti spice mix (page 26)
1 tbsp tomato purée
4 tomatoes, chopped
½ fresh green chilli, finely chopped
6 ladles of Balti sauce

Stage 1: Making Balti sauce

See page 24.

Stage 2: Balti method

Heat the oil in a large wok over high heat and fry the onions until just turning brown. Add the mince, garam masala, 1 tablespoon of the chopped coriander, the chilli powder, salt and methi. Stir-fry for 5 minutes, breaking up the lumps of mince as you do.

Add the garlic and butter. Stir-fry for another 2 minutes, then put in the spice mix, tomato purée, the rest of the chopped coriander, the chopped tomatoes, and green chilli. Stir-fry for another minute, breaking the tomatoes up.

Add 5 ladles of Balti sauce and the spinach. Turn the heat to low and simmer, still stirring, for 3 minutes. If the mixture gets too dry add a little more Balti sauce.

Divide among 4 warmed Balti bowls and serve.

HIGH QUALITY BALTI'S CHANA GOSHT (MEAT AND CHICK PEA) BALTI

(Proprietor and Chef Mr Begg)

The nutty flavour of chick peas works extremely well with the sweetness of lamb. Canned chick peas offer so much saving in time that Mr Begg recommends them rather than the dried variety.

3 Stages • Medium hot • Suitable for a family treat • Serves 4-6

*450 g / 1 lb boned lamb, cut into 4 cm /
   1¹/₂ inch cubes and par-cooked (using
   ingredients on page 22)*
*225 g / 8 oz dried chick peas, or use 425 g /
   15 oz can chick peas*
10 tbsp vegetable oil
4 onions, finely chopped
*4 cm / 1¹/₂ inch cube fresh ginger, peeled
   and grated*
6 garlic cloves, crushed
2 tsp chilli powder
1 tsp turmeric powder
2 tsp garam masala (page 25)
4 tbsp plain yoghurt
4 ladles of Balti sauce
2 small tomatoes, chopped
1 tbsp very finely chopped fresh coriander

Stage 1: Par-cooking the lamb and making the Balti sauce

See page 22, halving the ingredients.

Stage 2: Pre-cooking the chick peas

See page 24. Or open the can and drain well.

Stage 3: Balti method

Heat the oil in a large wok over moderate heat and fry the onions until brown. Add the ginger and garlic and stir-fry for 2 more minutes. Take the wok off the heat. Let it stand for a few minutes and then spoon off any excess oil.

Return the wok to a low heat. Sprinkle in the chilli powder, turmeric and 1 teaspoon of garam masala. Add the yoghurt 1 tablespoon at a time, stirring as you do so, and cook gently for 5 minutes. The sauce will turn to a reddish brown. Add the meat, the Balti sauce and the chick peas and stir them well in. Cover the wok and simmer for another 5 minutes.

Stir in the pieces of tomato (they are not supposed to cook properly). Divide among 4 warmed Balti bowls. Garnish each with a little chopped coriander and a pinch of garam masala, and serve.

IMRAN'S MUTTON KOFTA BALTI
(Proprietor and Chef Mr Butt)

These are delicious meatballs that are served unusually with hard-boiled eggs. This recipe is unusual in another way – it is one of very few in which the raw onions are squeezed of almost all their liquid before cooking. An uncomplicated recipe, this would suit a dinner party menu, and is simple enough for a family meal.

3 Stages • Subtly spiced • Serves 4

450 g / 1 lb minced mutton or lamb
900 g / 2 lb onions, grated and squeezed
    by hand so you end up with about
    225 g / 8 oz onion
2 fresh green chillies, very finely chopped
8 tbsp vegetable ghee or oil

^{1}/2 tsp ground ginger
^{1}/2 tsp garlic powder
1 tsp paprika
6 ladles of Balti sauce
2 eggs, hard-boiled and quartered
2 tsp chopped fresh coriander to garnish

Stage 1: Making the Balti sauce
See page 24.

Stage 2: Making the meatballs
Wet your hands so the mixture doesn't stick to them. Mash together the mince, squeezed onion and green chillies. Mould into balls about 4 cm / 1^1/2 inches in diameter.

Stage 3: Balti method
Heat the ghee or oil in a large wok over a high flame. Lower the meatballs in gently and roll them in the hot oil until they are browned all over. Add the ginger, garlic and paprika and stir them around, being careful not to break up the meatballs. Pour the Balti sauce over them and stir this gently too, making sure that each meatball is well covered. Cook and stir on the high flame for 15 minutes, then turn the heat down to low.

Add the egg quarters and stir them in gently. Cook for a further 2 minutes.

Divide the meatballs and sauce among 4 warmed Balti bowls and crown each bowl with hard-boiled egg. Garnish with a sprinkle of chopped coriander and serve.

KABABISH'S SAG GOSHT (LAMB AND SPINACH) BALTI
(Proprietor Mr Saddiqui, Chefs Mr Mir and Mr Afzal)

A darkly coloured and richly spiced dish that is suitable for a dinner party or when you just feel like celebrating. Salt, which seems to have an almost mythical quality in Balti cooking, 'helps to cook the meat', Mr Saddiqui says.

2 Stages • Medium hot • Serves 4

900 g / 2 lb boned leg of lamb, cut into
   2.5 cm / 1 inch cubes and par-cooked
   (using ingredients on page 22)
900 g / 2 lb fresh spinach, cooked and
   drained, or use 400 g / 14 oz frozen
   spinach, thawed and drained
5 tbsp vegetable oil
4 cm / 1½ inch cube fresh ginger, peeled
   and grated
4 garlic cloves, crushed

1 tsp ground black pepper
1½ tsp ground cumin
2 tsp ground coriander
1½ fresh green chillies, finely chopped
1½ tsp salt
6 ladles of Balti sauce
2 tomatoes, chopped
2 tbsp dried methi
1½ tsp garam masala (see page 25)
1 tbsp chopped fresh coriander

Stage 1: Par-cooking the lamb and making the Balti sauce
See page 22.

Stage 2: Balti method
In a large wok heat the oil over a high heat. Fry the ginger and garlic for 30 seconds. In quick succession add the pepper, cumin, ground coriander and chopped chillies. Stir and add the lamb and the salt. Stir vigorously and shake for 3 minutes to allow the spices time to infuse.

Add the Balti sauce, drained spinach, tomatoes and methi to the wok. Stir with a chopping motion to break up the tomato and to incorporate the spinach. Turn the heat down and simmer to reduce the sauce for a couple of minutes.

Divide among 4 warmed Balti bowls and serve, garnished with chopped coriander and a generous sprinkle of garam masala.

KABABISH'S VENISON BALTI
(Proprietor Mr Shafique, Chef Mr Khaliq)

A feast for a very grand occasion, this makes a wonderfully dark and very rich dish. We won't start with 'first catch one deer', although Mr Shafique has been known to do just that! The most discerning of guests would have to be impressed!

2 Stages • Medium spiced and very rich • Serves 4

FOR THE PAR-COOKING STAGE:
680 g / 1¹/₂ lb boned venison, cut into cubes
3 onions, roughly chopped
2 tsp salt
1 bouquet garni (page 26)
¹/₂ tsp chilli powder
¹/₄ tsp turmeric powder
FOR THE BALTI STAGE:
55 g / 2 oz slightly salted butter

3 cm / 1¹/₄ inch cube fresh ginger, peeled and grated
1 garlic clove, crushed
1 tsp dried methi
palmful of chopped fresh coriander, plus 2¹/₂ tsp to garnish
2 tomatoes, chopped
¹/₂ tsp ground cumin
¹/₂ tsp ground coriander
¹/₂ tsp garam masala to garnish (optional)

Stage 1: Par-cooking the venison and making the Balti sauce

Rinse the venison thoroughly and pat dry on kitchen paper. Put the venison and onions into a large saucepan with the salt, bouquet garni and 300 ml / ¹/₂ pint water. Braise with the lid on for 1-1¹/₂ hours over a very low heat, checking and stirring often to prevent the meat sticking or burning.

When the meat is just tender take it out with a slotted spoon and keep warm. Liquidise what is left in the pan and stir in the chilli powder and turmeric. This is your Balti sauce.

Stage 2: Balti method

In a large wok heat the butter and fry the ginger and garlic for 1 minute over high heat, stirring all the time. Pour in 5 ladles of the Balti sauce. In quick succession, still stirring, drop in the methi, fresh coriander, tomatoes, ground cumin and ground coriander. Add the venison and stir everything well together, turning the heat to low.

Check the moisture of the Balti. If it is too dry add a little more Balti sauce. Simmer for 10-15 minutes. When the butter separates the Balti is ready.

Divide among 4 warmed Balti bowls. Sprinkle a little chopped coriander over each and, if you like, a pinch of garam masala for its aroma.

KABABISH'S KIDNEY BALTI
(Proprietor Mr Saddiqui, Chef Mr Khaliq)

Kidneys were made for Balti-ing! This recipe makes a thick dark brown sauce. It is very rich, especially if you, like Mr Khaliq, use butter. Calf kidneys would transform it into a luxury meal. Halve the amount of chilli if authenticity isn't your main aim!

1 Stage • Fairly hot • A family dish • Serves 4

12 lambs' kidneys, skinned, cut in half and cored
115 g / 4 oz butter or 8 tbsp vegetable oil
salt to taste
3 onions, chopped
2 tsp turmeric powder
4-5 fresh green chillies or 1-1½ tsp chilli powder

a small piece of fresh ginger, peeled and grated
2 garlic cloves, crushed
½ tsp ground cumin
½ tsp ground coriander
1 tsp paprika
2-3 brown cardamoms, broken slightly open
chopped fresh coriander to garnish

Heat half the butter or oil in a large wok over moderate heat. Season the kidneys with salt and fry them for about 5 minutes, turning them frequently to brown them on all sides without burning. Lift the kidneys from the wok and keep to one side.

Put the other half of the butter or oil into the wok. When it is hot fry the onions until they are soft and turning translucent. Add all the other ingredients, except the kidneys, and cook, stirring frequently, for 3 minutes. If the sauce is getting too dry add a little water.

Put in the kidneys and cook for 10 more minutes, stirring all the time. Watch for too much drying out. The sauce is supposed to be quite thick. Adjust the seasoning.

Divide among 4 warmed Balti bowls and serve, garnished with chopped coriander. Eat with naan bread.

KHAN'S LAMB PATHIA BALTI

(Proprietor Mr Khan, Chef Mr 'A.N. Other' Khan)

Hot, sour and sweet.

2 Stages • Good for a family meal as long as everyone has a taste for spicy food • Serves 4

900 g / 2 lb boned lamb, cut into 3 cm / 1¼ inch cubes and par-cooked (using ingredients on page 22)
6 tbsp vegetable oil
4 cm / 1½ inch cube fresh ginger, peeled and grated
6 garlic cloves, crushed
2 onions, chopped
2 fresh green chillies, seeded and chopped

1 green pepper, seeded and diced
3 tomatoes, chopped
2 tsp tomato purée
5 tsp Balti spice mix (page 26)
3 tbsp lemon juice
1 tbsp sugar
5-6 ladles of Balti sauce
salt to taste
garam masala to garnish

Stage 1: Par-cooking the lamb and making the Balti sauce

See page 22.

Stage 2: Balti method

Heat the oil in a large wok over a moderate heat and stir-fry the ginger and garlic for 1 minute. Add the onions and fry until soft. Stir in the chillies, diced pepper, tomatoes and tomato purée. Add the spice mix, lemon juice, sugar and 5 ladles of Balti sauce.

Put in the pieces of lamb and add salt to taste. Cook, stirring all the time, for 5 minutes. Adjust the moisture by adding more Balti sauce, or by reducing the mixture on high heat. Adjust the seasoning.

Divide among 4 warmed Balti bowls and serve, aromatised with a sprinkle of garam masala.

KHYBER'S KEEMA DAL (MINCED LAMB AND SPLIT PEA) BALTI

(Proprietor Mr Sarwar, Chefs Mrs Sarwar and Mr A. Rais)

The delicately spiced, finely minced lamb contrasts nicely with the yellow dots of slightly crunchy split peas and the green slivers of pepper. It's a wholesome dish mild enough for children. The head chef talked us through the stages of this Balti. Mrs Sarwar, formerly a mathematics teacher, cooked with delicate poise and grace.

3 Stages • Mild • Serves 4

680 g / 1½ lb finely minced lamb
225 g / 8 oz yellow split peas
½ tsp turmeric powder
¾-1 tsp salt

FOR THE BALTI STAGE:
6 tbsp vegetable oil
4 cm / 1½ inch cube fresh ginger, peeled and grated

6 garlic cloves, crushed
½ tsp chilli powder
½ tsp salt
1 large green pepper, seeded and thinly sliced
1 litre / 1¾ pints Balti sauce (Rolls Royce version, page 25)
1 heaped tsp garam masala (page 25)
2 tbsp chopped fresh coriander

Stage 1: Pre-cooking the yellow split peas

See page 24; use the turmeric and salt.

Stage 2: Making the Balti sauce

See page 25.

Stage 3: Balti method

Heat the oil in a large wok over a moderately high flame. Stir-fry the ginger and garlic for half a minute. Now put in the minced lamb, the chilli powder, salt and green pepper. Stir and fry for 5 minutes, breaking up lumps of meat with the side of the spoon.

Pour in the Balti sauce and stir everything well. Add the split peas, garam masala and chopped coriander. Turn the heat to low, cover the wok and simmer for a further 10 minutes.

Divide among 4 warmed Balti bowls and serve.

MEMSAHIB'S GOSHT (LAMB) MASALA BALTI
(Proprietors Mr and Mrs A. and S. O'Flaherty, Chef Mr Yassim)

Lamb grilled, ideally over charcoal, in a spicy sauce. The barbecue-ness of the lamb elbows its way, politely, through the quite strong spice of the sauce.

4 Stages • Mild • A family meal • Serves 4

680 g / 1¹/₂ lb boned lamb, cubed and
   par-cooked
300 ml / ¹/₂ pint plain yoghurt
3 tbsp lemon juice
1¹/₂ tbsp garlic powder
2 tsp salt

3 tsp garam masala (page 25)
8 tbsp vegetable oil
2 tomatoes, quartered
3 tbsp chopped fresh coriander
8 ladles of Balti sauce
1¹/₂ tsp dried methi

Stage 1: Marinading the lamb
(Prepare the night before.) In a large bowl mix together the yoghurt, lemon juice, 1 tablespoon of the garlic powder, the salt and 2 teaspoons of garam masala. Stir the meat into this, making sure that each piece is well covered. Cover the bowl with cling film and chill overnight, if possible, or for at least 6 hours.

Stage 2: Making the Balti sauce
See page 24.

Stage 3: Grilling the lamb
Take the pieces of lamb from the marinade and thread them on to skewers. Put them on the barbecue or under a hot grill and cook them for 8-10 minutes, turning from time to time, until they are brown on the outside but still a little rare in the middle.

Slide the pieces of lamb off the skewers and set aside.

Stage 4: Balti method
Heat the oil in a large wok over a moderately high heat. Fry the tomatoes, breaking them up with the side of the spoon. Add the fresh coriander and the rest of the garlic powder. Stir-fry for about 1 minute and then add the Balti sauce. Stir well. Put in the methi and lamb. Cook, stirring constantly, for 5 minutes.

Divide among 4 warmed Balti bowls. Aromatise with the remaining garam masala and serve with naan bread.

THE MINAR'S CHUTNEY KOFTA (MEATBALLS) BALTI

(Proprietors the Mohammed brothers, Chef M. Sohel)

'Chutney' does not mean chutney as we know it. It seems to be a mis-translation of 'chhote kofte'. They are anyway delicious meatballs in spicy sauce.

3 Stages • Fairly hot • Ideal for a family meal • Serves 4

450 g / 1 lb lean minced lamb
4 onions, finely chopped
2 fresh green chillies, finely chopped
1 tsp crushed dried chillies, or use 1/2 tsp chilli powder
1 tsp salt
3 1/2 tbsp chopped fresh coriander
1/2 tsp mango powder (amchur)

vegetable oil for frying meatballs, plus 5 tbsp for the Balti stage
4 ladles of Balti sauce
4 cm / 1 1/2 inch cube fresh ginger, peeled and grated
8 large garlic cloves, crushed
1 1/2 tbsp dried methi
1 tsp tandoori masala powder

Stage 1: Making the Balti sauce
See page 24.

Stage 2: Making the meatballs
Wet your hands so the mixture won't stick to them. Mix together the mince, half of the chopped onions, the fresh chillies, dried chillies or chilli powder, salt, 1 1/2 tablespoons of fresh coriander and the mango powder. Make into meatballs 4 cm / 1 1/2 inches in diameter.

Fry in hot oil for 8 minutes, turning them often so they brown on all sides. Drain on kitchen paper.

Stage 3: Balti method
Heat the 5 tablespoons of oil in a large wok over moderate heat. Fry the rest of the onions until lightly browned. Add the meatballs and Balti sauce and stir. Add, in quick succession, the rest of the chopped coriander, ginger, methi, garlic and tandoori masala. Cook for 10 minutes, stirring gently. The dish should be quite dry to be authentic.

Divide the meatballs among 4 warmed Balti bowls. Ladle the sauce over each and serve.

MR DAVE'S ALOO GOSHT (LAMB AND POTATO) BALTI

(Manager Qamar Zaman, Chef Habib Hussain, Assistant Manager Sajad, 'Saj' for short, Karim)

A Balti that's delicious and warming, rather like a spicy version of a good old English casserole. No need for Balti sauce as the dish makes its own.

3 Stages • Hot • A filling family meal to be tucked into on a cold day • Serves 4

450 g / 1 lb boned lamb, cut into 3 cm / 1¼ inch cubes and par-cooked (using the ingredients from page 22)

900 g / 2 lb potatoes, peeled

8 tbsp vegetable oil

2 onions, grated or really finely chopped

2-3 tsp chilli powder

2 tsp turmeric powder

2 tsp garam masala (page 25)

2 tsp paprika

1-2 tsp salt

2.5 cm / 1 inch cube fresh ginger, peeled and grated

10 garlic cloves, crushed

4 tomatoes, chopped

3 ladles of Balti sauce

1 tsp dried methi

chopped fresh coriander to garnish

Stage 1: Par-cooking the meat and making the Balti sauce
See page 22, halving the ingredients.

Stage 2: Par-cooking the potatoes
Cook the potatoes in boiling salted water for 10–15 minutes. Drain when they still retain some of their crunch. Cut into cubes.

Stage 3: Balti method
In a large wok heat the oil over a high flame. Fry the onions until they are turning golden brown. Stirring vigorously, put in the chilli powder, turmeric, garam masala, paprika and salt. Moisten with the ginger, garlic and tomatoes, stirring, then put in the pieces of lamb and the Balti sauce. Make sure the lamb is well coated with the spices. Turn the heat to low. If the mixture is too dry add a little water. Cook for 4 minutes.

Put in the potatoes. Stir-fry for a further 10 minutes. Adjust the salt or chilli powder if necessary, and taste a little meat and potato to make sure they're cooked. Stir in the methi and immediately remove from the heat.

Divide among 4 warmed Balti bowls, garnish with a sprinkle of chopped coriander and serve.

PANJAB TANDOORI'S KEEMA (MINCED LAMB) BALTI
(Proprietor and Chef Kailash Watts)

A good basic Balti. If you happen to have some Balti sauce in the freezer it is so simple you could spoil yourself and make it dinner for one, or two. (Divide the ingredients, though!)

2 Stages • Medium • Suitable for a family meal • Serves 4

900 g / 2 lb minced lamb
150 g / 5¹/2 oz butter
3 onions, chopped
¹/2 green pepper, seeded and diced
4 cm / 1¹/2 inch cube fresh ginger, peeled
    and grated
7 garlic cloves, crushed
5 ladles of Balti sauce

5 tsp Balti spice mix (page 26)
1¹/2 tbsp dried methi
2 fresh green chillies, seeded and finely
    chopped
3 tbsp chopped fresh coriander
2 small tomatoes, chopped
4 tbsp milk

Stage 1: Making the Balti sauce
See page 24.

Stage 2: Balti method
Melt the butter in a large wok over a moderate heat. When hot stir-fry the onions and green pepper for about 5 minutes. Add the ginger, garlic and the minced lamb. Stir and shake vigorously, breaking up the lumps of mince as you do.

When the mince is browned all over add the Balti sauce, spice mix, and all the other ingredients. Stir-fry for 4-5 more minutes.

Divide among 4 warmed Balti bowls and serve.

PLAZA'S BHOLA (LAMB AND CHICKEN) BALTI
(Proprietor and Chef Mr R.S. 'Ravi' Ghataera)

A complex combination of chicken and lamb and, in Ravi's case, five different vegetables. You could use just two vegetables you like, or use up any left-over vegetables. The use of spring onions gives a quite different, more peppery taste than ordinary onions.

4 Stages • Subtly spiced • A dinner party recipe • Serves 4-6

680 g / 1¹/2 lb chicken pieces, pre-cooked
   (using the ingredients from page 22)
450 g / 1 lb boned lamb, cut into 2.5 cm /
   1 inch cubes and par-cooked (using the
   ingredients from page 22)
2 potatoes, peeled
2 small carrots
¹/2 cauliflower, broken into florets
1 aubergine, cut into small cubes
115 g / 4 oz shelled fresh or frozen peas
6 tbsp vegetable oil

4 cm / 1¹/2 inch cube fresh ginger, peeled
   and grated
8 garlic cloves, crushed
3 tbsp chopped spring onions
3 tomatoes, chopped
4-6 ladles of Balti sauce
2 tsp salt
2 tsp paprika
1 tsp turmeric powder
1¹/2 tbsp chopped fresh coriander
¹/2 tsp garam masala (see page 25)

Stage 1: Par-cooking the lamb and making the Balti sauce
See page 22, halving the ingredients.

Stage 2: Pre-cooking the chicken and making the Balti sauce
See page 22, halving the ingredients.

Stage 3: Par-cooking the vegetables
See page 23. After draining, cut the potatoes into 1 cm / ¹/2 inch cubes.

Stage 4: Balti method
There are a lot of ingredients in this dish and we suggest that you will find it easier to cook in two goes. Make sure you use HALF of each ingredient for each batch.

(While the first batch is simmering, make the second.)

Use your largest wok. Over a moderately high flame heat the oil and fry the ginger and garlic for 30 seconds. Add the spring onions and tomatoes. Stir and fry for 2 minutes, breaking up the tomatoes with the side of the spoon.

Add the pre-cooked chicken, lamb, vegetables and 2-3 ladles of the chicken and lamb Balti sauces. Add the salt, paprika and turmeric. Stir everything well. Turn the heat very low, cover with a lid and simmer gently for 4 minutes.

Divide among 4 or 6 warmed Balti bowls, garnish with the coriander and garam masala, and serve.

PUNJAB PARADISE'S LAMB KORMA BALTI

(Proprietor Mr Shabaz, Chef Pinnu Khan, Head waiter 'Tan'
Tanveer Choudry, who gave us this recipe)

'Korma' is a sweet nutty-tasting sauce punctuated with sultanas. This dish is cooked from scratch in the Balti.

2 Stages • A family dish (children especially will love it) • Serves 4

680 g / 1½ lb boned lamb, cubed
FOR THE KORMA:
2 tbsp desiccated coconut
2 tbsp sultanas
1 tbsp sugar
2 tbsp plain yoghurt
2-3 tsp evaporated milk
FOR THE BALTI STAGE:
5 tbsp vegetable oil

3 onions, finely chopped
4 tomatoes, chopped
1 tsp ground cumin
1 tsp ground coriander
1 tsp garam masala (page 25)
½ tsp chilli powder
½ green pepper, seeded and diced
¼ tsp salt
6 tbsp chopped fresh coriander

Stage 1: Making the korma

Simply mix all the ingredients in a small bowl, dribbling in the evaporated milk gradually at the end so that you don't make the sauce too runny.

Stage 2: Balti method

Heat the oil in a large wok over a high flame. Put in the onions and fry them until they are translucent. Add the tomatoes and, stirring all the time, add the cumin, ground coriander, garam masala, chilli powder, the green pepper, salt and chopped coriander. Pour in 450 ml / ¾ pint of water.

Add the cubes of lamb. Stir well. Bring to the boil, then turn the heat to low, cover with a lid and simmer gently for 35-45 minutes. Check occasionally whether you need to add more water, and stir from time to time.

When the meat is just tender add the korma sauce. Stir this well in and cook for 5 more minutes.

Divide among 4 warmed Balti dishes and serve.

ROYAL AL-FAISAL'S KEEMA KARELA BALTI
(Proprietor Mr Muhammad Ajaib)

Karelas are also called 'bitter gourd' and, it must be admitted, are an acquired taste. They need to be salted and left to drain for 5-6 hours, but they have such a distinctive flavour that they are worth the time. Make sure you have plenty of paprika on the shelf before you start this rich dish.

4 Stages • Medium hot • A dinner party dish for guests with adventurous tastes • Serves 4

900 g / 2 lb minced lamb, minced again in a food processor
450 g / 1 lb fresh karela, or use canned karela
salt
6 onions, 4 chopped, 2 thinly sliced
7 tbsp vegetable oil
1 bouquet garni (page 26)
1 1/2 tbsp turmeric powder

6 tbsp paprika
2 1/2 tsp chilli powder
5 tomatoes, chopped
2 fresh green chillies, finely chopped
handful of chopped fresh coriander
2 tsp dried methi, ground in a mortar
1 tsp garlic powder
1 tsp garam masala (page 25)

Stage 1: Preparing the karela
Grate the skin off so the surface is roughly smooth. (Most of the bitterness is in the skin so this should be done thoroughly.) Cut into slices about 2 cm / 3/4 inch thick and remove any of the seeds that have gone hard. Rub the slices with plenty of salt and place them on a plate. Prop up one side of the plate so that the bitter juices can run off. Leave to drain for 5-6 hours.

If using canned karela, drain it well and slice it if necessary.

Stage 2: Making the Balti sauce
Put the chopped onions into a large saucepan and add 1.2 litres / 2 pints

water. Bring to the boil. Cook gently until the onions are soft. Let them cool and then liquidise them.

Wipe the pan clean with kitchen paper and heat 4 tablespoons of the oil. Put the onion purée back into the pan and the bouquet garni, 1 teaspoon of salt, 1 tablespoon of turmeric, 4 1/2 tablespoons of paprika and 2 teaspoons of chilli powder (this is optional). Stir. Cook gently, stirring at first and then with the lid on, for 30-45 minutes. Taste after 20 minutes to see if the sauce is spicy enough. Critical judgment is needed to know when to remove the bouquet garni.

Mr Ajaib stresses the importance of the

Balti sauce to the finished dish and says that what you should aim for is when the 'onion taste' has gone and the overall taste is 'one' (a bit Zen?). He then comes down more to earth. 'When the bitter taste of the onions has been killed, this is "gravy"!'

Stage 3: Par-cooking the mince and karela

In a large frying pan heat 3 tablespoons of vegetable oil. Fry the 2 sliced onions on low heat until they are just starting to go brown. Add 2 of the chopped tomatoes, stirring them in. Add the chillies and remaining turmeric, paprika and chilli powder. Fry all this, stirring and breaking up the tomatoes, for about 2 minutes. Add the minced lamb and cook until browned all over, breaking up lumps with the spoon.

Wash the salt off the karela slices and pat them dry on kitchen paper. Turn the heat to low and add the karela to the frying pan. Cook gently, turning the slices, until they are just tender. Remove from the heat and keep warm.

Stage 4: Balti method

Take 1¹/₂ tablespoons of oil (ideally from the top of the Balti sauce, which is nicely infused with spices) and heat it in a large wok. Put in the chopped coriander and almost immediately add 5 ladles of the Balti sauce. Stir together. Sprinkle on to this the ground methi and garlic powder. Add the remaining chopped tomatoes, and break them up as you stir-cook. Add another ladle of the Balti sauce and stir and cook until the aroma of the garlic comes out (about 3 minutes).

Put in the mince and karela, with any more Balti sauce if you need to, and heat through for 2 minutes.

Divide among 4 warmed Balti bowls and sprinkle a very little garam masala on each.

ROYAL WATAN'S KEEMA DOPIAZA (MINCED LAMB AND ONIONS) BALTI

(Proprietor Mr M. Akram, Chef Mohammed Younis)

A classic Balti dish. Dopiaza means '2 onions' – some soft and integrated into the sauce and some fried and added later.

2 Stages • Mild • Suitable for a family meal • Serves 4

680 g / 1½ lb minced lamb
8 tbsp vegetable oil
4 onions, 2 finely sliced, 2 chopped
4 cm / 1½ inch cube fresh ginger, peeled
  and grated
8 garlic cloves, crushed
4 tomatoes, roughly chopped

2 tsp paprika
2 tsp turmeric powder
½ tsp chilli powder
2 tsp ground cumin
2 tsp ground coriander
6 ladles of Balti sauce
2 tbsp chopped fresh coriander

Stage 1: Making the Balti sauce
See page 24.

Stage 2: Balti method
Heat the oil in a large wok over moderately high heat and fry the sliced onions. When they are brown remove them with a slotted spoon and keep to one side.

Put in the chopped onions and fry until translucent. Add the ginger, garlic and tomatoes. Stir, breaking up the tomatoes with the spoon as you do. Add the paprika, turmeric, chilli powder, and ground cumin and coriander. Stir well and put in the mince. Stir-fry for 5 minutes, breaking up the lumps of mince.

Add the Balti sauce and cook, still stirring, for 3 minutes. Stir in the chopped coriander and the fried onions. Turn the heat to low and simmer for 2 more minutes.

Divide among 4 warmed Balti bowls and serve.

ROYAL WATAN'S LAMB, DAL (SPLIT PEA) AND VEGETABLE BALTI

(Proprietor Mr M. Akram, Chef Mohammed Younis)

This is a good down to earth dish that combines lamb with any vegetables you may have to hand.

4 Stages • Mild • Suitable for a family meal • Serves 4

900 g / 2 lb boned lamb, cut into 4 cm / 1½ inch cubes and par-cooked (using ingredients on page 22)
170 g / 6 oz yellow split peas
400 g / 14 oz prepared mixed vegetables: dried or canned red kidney beans, ladies' fingers (okra), potatoes, shelled fresh or frozen peas, spinach, mushrooms, in any combination you like
5 tbsp vegetable oil
2 onions, chopped

4 cm / 1½ inch cube fresh ginger, peeled and grated
8 garlic cloves, crushed
4 tomatoes, roughly chopped
2 tsp paprika
2 tsp turmeric powder
½ tsp chilli powder
2 tsp ground cumin
2 tsp ground coriander
6 ladles of Balti sauce
2 tbsp chopped fresh coriander

Stage 1. Par-cooking the lamb and making the Balti sauce
See page 22.

Stage 2: Pre-cooking the split peas
See page 24.

Stage 3: Par-cooking the vegetables
For fresh vegetables, see page 23; cook with the salt but without spices. After draining, cut the potatoes into cubes. For pre-cooking dried kidney beans, see page 24. Drain all canned vegetables.

Stage 4: Balti method
Heat the oil in a large wok over a moderately high flame. Fry the onions until they are translucent, then add the ginger, garlic and tomatoes. Stir, breaking up the tomatoes with the spoon as you do. Add the paprika, turmeric, chilli powder, and the ground cumin and coriander. Stir well.

Put in the lamb. Make sure that it is well covered by the mixture before you ladle in the Balti sauce. Stir-fry for 3 minutes. Add the cooked split peas and the par-cooked vegetables and stir-fry for another 3 minutes.

Stir in 1½ tablespoons of chopped coriander. Turn the heat to low and after another minute remove from the heat.

Divide among 4 warmed Balti bowls and serve garnished with the rest of the chopped coriander.

RUBY'S LAHORI BALTI
(Proprietor and Chef Mr Ahmed)

Ruby's menu describes this as 'hot'. It is of grown-up strength and sophistication. It gives a pleasant tingling around the lips from the green chilli, with the subtlety that chilli powder sometimes lacks. One of the stages is the grilling of lamb chops, or barbecueing them. The temptation is to stop at this point! But the Balti stage is well worth the small extra effort.

4 Stages • Hot • Serves 4

8 thinly cut lamb chops
2 x 2.5 cm / 1 inch cubes fresh ginger,
    peeled and grated
6 garlic cloves, crushed
1 heaped tbsp dried methi
3 tbsp chopped fresh coriander
1/2 tsp lovage seeds (ajwan), optional

300 ml / 1/2 pint plain yoghurt
3 tbsp vegetable ghee or oil
4 onions, chopped
1 green pepper, seeded and chopped
4 fresh long, thin, green chillies, finely
    chopped
6 ladles of Balti sauce

Stage 1: Marinading the chops
In a large bowl, mix half the ginger and garlic, the methi, 2 tablespoons of chopped coriander and the lovage seeds into the yoghurt. Put the lamb chops into the spiced yoghurt and stir them around so that each becomes thoroughly covered in marinade. Cover the bowl with cling film and leave in the fridge for a minimum of 2 hours (overnight is always better).

Stage 2: Making the Balti sauce
See page 24.

Stage 3: Grilling or barbecueing the lamb chops
Remove the chops from the bowl, shaking off most of the marinade. (You could freeze the remaining marinade and re-use it later.) Grill or barbecue the chops until they are still pink in the middle.

Stage 4: Balti method
Heat the oil in a large wok over a high flame and fry the onions and green pepper until the onions are translucent. Add the rest of the ginger and garlic and the chillies. Stir these around and pour in 4 ladles of Balti sauce.

Now put in the lamb chops. Cook, stirring and occasionally turning the chops over in the sauce, for 6-7 minutes or until they are cooked inside. The finished sauce should be quite thick. You may have to turn the heat up for the last few minutes to reduce it, or add more Balti sauce to moisten the dish.

Divide among 4 warmed Balti bowls and serve garnished with the remaining chopped coriander.

RUBY'S ROGAN JOSH (LAMB) BALTI
(Proprietor and Chef Mr Ahmed)

A delicious Balti that's very pleasing to the eye. The peppers are dark green, the onions creamy coloured, all wrapped in a terracotta-coloured sauce.

2 Stages • Mildly spiced • A Balti for entertaining • Serves 4

FOR THE PAR-COOKING STAGE:
900 g / 2 lb boned lamb, cut into 2.5 cm /
    1 inch cubes
4 tbsp vegetable oil
4 onions, diced
1½ tbsp paprika
2 tsp chilli powder
5 tsp Balti spice mix (page 26)
2 tsp turmeric powder
5 brown cardamoms, broken slightly open
5 whole cloves
FOR THE BALTI STAGE:
3 tbsp vegetable oil

1 onion, diced
3 cm / 1¼ inch cube fresh ginger, peeled
    and grated
5 garlic cloves, crushed
½ green pepper, seeded and diced
1 tbsp lemon juice
150 ml / ¼ pint plain yoghurt
1 tsp curry powder
2 tsp each yellow and red food colouring
    (optional)
TO GARNISH:
2 tsp chopped fresh coriander
½ tsp garam masala

Stage 1: Par-cooking the lamb and making the Balti sauce

Heat the oil in a large saucepan over a moderate flame and fry the diced onions until translucent. Add the cubes of lamb, the paprika, chilli powder, Balti spice mix, turmeric, cardamoms, cloves and 300 ml/ ½ pint water. Bring to the boil. Cover the pan, turn the heat to low and simmer for 1 hour or until the lamb is tender but still pink in the middle.

Remove the lamb cubes with a slotted spoon and set aside. Pour the contents of the pan into a blender or food processor and liquidise. This is your Balti sauce.

Stage 2: Balti method

Heat the oil in a wok over a high flame. Fry the onion until it starts to change colour. Set aside a teaspoon each of the ginger and garlic. Put the rest into the wok with the green pepper, lemon juice, lamb cubes and the Balti sauce. Cook, stirring, for 5 minutes. In a small bowl mix together the yoghurt, the reserved ginger and garlic, the curry powder and food colouring. Stir this mixture into the wok, turn the heat to low and cook for 7 minutes.

Divide among 4 warmed Balti bowls. Garnish with chopped coriander and garam masala and serve.

SALEEM'S KEEMA CHANA (MINCED LAMB AND CHICK PEA) BALTI

(Proprietor and Chef Mr Rafiq)

A classic Baltihouse favourite. A very good simple dish that you can bribe the family with, or for when you just want to please them.

2 Stages • Mild-Medium hot • Serves 4

340 g / 3/4 lb minced lamb
200 g / 7 oz dried chick peas, or use
   canned
5 tbsp vegetable oil
2 onions, finely chopped
3 tomatoes, roughly chopped
5 tsp Balti spice mix (page 26)
1 tsp turmeric powder

1/2 green pepper, seeded and diced
1 fresh green chilli, finely chopped
2.5 cm / 1 inch cube fresh ginger, peeled
   and grated
5 large garlic cloves, crushed
3/4 tsp garam masala (see page 25)
1/2 tsp salt
1 tbsp chopped fresh coriander

Stage 1: Pre-cooking the chick peas
See page 24. Or open the can and drain well.

Stage 2: Balti method
Heat the oil in a large wok on a moderately high heat and stir-fry the onions until they are translucent. Put in the tomatoes, Balti sauce mix, turmeric, green pepper, chilli and minced lamb. Stir with gusto, breaking up the mince and tomatoes. As the meat starts to brown, pour in most of a measured 150 ml / 1/4 pint water and bring to the boil. Add the ginger and garlic, turn the heat to low and simmer for 20 minutes. If the sauce gets too dry add a little more water.

Add the chick peas, garam masala, salt and coriander and bring back to the boil. Cook on a low heat, stirring occasionally, for about 5 minutes, adding more water if it gets too dry again. Check the seasoning.

Divide among 4 warmed Balti bowls and serve. This is the kind of dish that's even nicer eaten with chapatis.

SHAHENSHAH'S GUJRANWALA LAMB BALTI

(Proprietor Mr Ayub)

A superb spicy lamb Balti. It is unusual in that the recipe comes directly from the town of the same name on the Punjab/Kashmir border, and wasn't developed in Birmingham.

2 Stages • Spicy · For impressing dinner guests • Serves 4

900 g / 2 lb boned lamb, cubed
8 onions, 5 chopped, 3 thinly sliced
2$\frac{1}{2}$ fresh green chillies, finely chopped
2 tsp curry powder
4 tsp ground coriander
$\frac{3}{4}$ tsp salt
1$\frac{1}{4}$ tsp garam masala (page 25)
7 tbsp vegetable oil

4 cm / 1$\frac{1}{2}$ inch cube fresh ginger, peeled
   and grated
4 large garlic cloves, crushed
2 tomatoes, chopped
2 green peppers, seeded and diced
1 tsp chilli powder
2 tsp paprika
5 tbsp dried methi, rubbed between your
   hands

Stage 1: Par-cooking the lamb and making the Balti sauce

Put the lamb, 3 of the chopped onions and $\frac{1}{2}$ a green chilli into a saucepan. Add 300 ml / $\frac{1}{2}$ pint water and bring to the boil. Add half the curry powder and ground coriander, the salt and $\frac{1}{2}$ teaspoon of garam masala. Cover the pan, reduce the heat and simmer for 1 hour or until the lamb is tender. Remove the meat with a slotted spoon and set aside.

Heat 1 tablespoon oil in another large saucepan and fry the remaining chopped onions until soft and translucent. Add the liquid from cooking the lamb and another 150 ml / $\frac{1}{4}$ pint water and bring to the boil.

After 10 minutes add the rest of the curry powder, ground coriander and garam masala and simmer for 5 minutes.

Remove from the heat, pour into a blender or food processor and liquidise. This is now the Balti sauce.

Stage 2: Balti method

Heat the remaining oil in a large wok over moderately high heat. When it is hot stir-fry the ginger and garlic for 1 minute. Then put in the sliced onions and fry them until they are starting to soften. Add, in quick succession, stirring and shaking all the time, the tomatoes, the rest of the chillies, the green peppers, chilli powder, paprika, methi and 5 ladles of Balti sauce. Stir well and add the meat. Turn the heat down and simmer for 15 minutes, stirring gently from time to time.

Divide among 4 warmed Balti bowls and serve with naan bread.

SHEEREEN KADAH'S KEEMA, SAG AND CHANA (MINCED LAMB, SPINACH AND CHICK PEAS) BALTI

(Proprietor Jimmy Khan, Chef Hasan Baba)

A combination of three classic Balti ingredients.

3 Stages • Spicy • Suitable for any Balti occasion • Serves 4

680 g / 1¹/₂ lb minced lamb
570 g / 1¹/₄ lb fresh spinach, cooked and
    drained, or use 400 g / 14 oz frozen,
    thawed and drained
100 g / 3¹/₂ oz dried chick peas, or use
    canned
4 tbsp vegetable oil
2 tsp cumin seeds
¹/₂ tsp mustard seeds
2 onions, chopped
1 fresh green chilli, finely chopped
3 cm / 1¹/₄ inch cube fresh ginger, peeled
    and grated

1 tsp turmeric powder
2 tsp ground coriander
1 tomato, roughly chopped
4 garlic cloves, crushed
6 ladles of Balti sauce
1¹/₂ tbsp chopped fresh coriander
1-2 tsp salt
2 palmfuls of dried methi, rubbed between
    your hands
¹/₂ tsp garam masala (page 25)
¹/₄ tsp chilli powder

Stage 1: Pre-cooking the chick peas
See page 24. Or open the can and drain well.

Stage 2: Making the Balti sauce
See page 24.

Stage 3: Balti method
Heat half of the oil in a large wok over moderate heat. Put in the cumin and mustard seeds and fry until they start to pop. Add the onions, green chilli, half the ginger, the turmeric and ground coriander. Stir-fry until the onions are translucent.

Add the mince and fry, stirring and breaking up the lumps of meat, until it is browned all over. Put in the rest of the oil and ginger, the tomato, garlic and Balti sauce. Stir-fry for 3 minutes.

Add the chopped coriander, keeping a little for garnish, 1 teaspoon of salt, the methi, garam masala and chilli powder. Stir well. Add the spinach and chick peas. Stir-fry for 3 more minutes or until everything is well heated through. Taste and add more salt if you like.

Divide among 4 warmed Balti bowls and serve garnished with a sprinkle of chopped coriander.

SHER KHAN'S MUTTON BALTI
(Chef Mr Saeed)

Mr Saeed insists that you get by far the best taste if you use mutton not lamb, and par-cook the meat on the bone, removing the bone before Balti-ing. This is a wonderfully rich dish with a strong influence of methi.

2 Stages • Mildly spiced • Suitable for the family or for entertaining • Serves 4–6

FOR THE PAR-COOKING STAGE:
about 1.15 kg / 2¹/₂ lb leg of mutton,
*   with the bone*
2 onions, chopped
3 tbsp vegetable oil
2 small tomatoes, chopped
1¹/₂ tbsp Balti spice mix (page 26)
2 tsp turmeric powder
¹/₃ green pepper, seeded and chopped

FOR THE BALTI STAGE:
6 tbsp vegetable oil
2.5 cm / 1 inch cube fresh ginger, peeled
*   and grated*
4 garlic cloves, crushed
4 small tomatoes, chopped
¹/₂ tsp chilli powder
3 tbsp dried methi
1 tsp garam masala (page 25)

Stage 1: Par-cooking the mutton and making the Balti sauce

See page 22, allowing more time for par-cooking than you would with lamb. Use the ingredients above, with 300 ml / ¹/₂ pint water. When the mutton is cool enough to handle, remove the meat from the bones and cut it into cubes.

Stage 2: Balti method

Make sure you have all the ingredients around the stove so you can work really fast.

With your wok on a moderate flame heat the oil. When it's sizzling hot, spoon in the ginger and garlic and 4 ladles of the Balti sauce. Add the tomatoes. Stir-fry, breaking them up. Now add the cubes of meat. Stir them around so that they get completely covered in Balti sauce.

Then, stirring like mad, quickly add the chilli powder, methi and garam masala. Cook fast and stir constantly until the oil separates (about 7–10 minutes).

Divide among 4 warmed Balti bowls and serve, with chapatis or naan bread.

SPICE VALLEY'S GUSHTABBA BALTI

(Proprietor Mr Alom, Chef Nazir Ahmed)

The sourish taste of the combined coriander and chilli makes these spicy meatballs hot without being unkind. Mr Ahmed is a joy to watch. You can taste his love of food and cooking, after one bite of Gushtabba. This is definitely a dish for a Saturday night treat or a dinner party. Adjust quantities for more servings, but don't try to cook for more than 4 people at one time.

3 Stages • Quite hot • Serves 4

680 g / 1¹/2 lb minced lamb
4 onions, finely chopped
3 handfuls of chopped fresh coriander
5 tbsp dried methi
1 tbsp garam masala (page 25)
5 tsp Balti spice mix (page 26)
1 tsp turmeric powder
1 tbsp salt
1 tsp chilli powder
2 eggs
1 heaped tbsp gram flour
3 tbsp cumin seeds, rubbed between your hands

3 fresh long, thin, green chillies, very thinly sliced
6 slices of lemon
4 tbsp vegetable ghee or oil
2.5 cm / 1 inch cube fresh ginger, peeled and grated
6 large garlic cloves, crushed
1 green pepper, seeded and finely chopped
2 tsp tomato purée
6 tomatoes, chopped

Stage 1: Making the meatballs

In a large mixing bowl combine the minced lamb, 2 of the onions, 2 handfuls of the coriander, 4 tablespoons of methi, 1 teaspoon of garam masala, the Balti spice mix, turmeric, 2 teaspoons of salt and the chilli powder. Break the eggs over all this. Add the gram flour (there's no need to sift it) and rub in 2 tablespoons of the cumin seeds. Knead the mixture until well mixed. Add 1 of the green chillies and knead again. When all the ingredients are perfectly integrated leave the mixture to stand for 5 minutes.

Wet your hands to prevent the mixture sticking and roll into balls 3 cm / 1¹/4 inches in diameter.

Stage 2: Cooking the meatballs

Bring a large saucepan of water to the boil. Drop the lemon slices in and turn the heat down until the water is just simmering. Lower the meatballs in gently one at a time. The aim is to cook them surreptitiously for 5 minutes and then turn the heat up and boil them for 7 more minutes. This process prevents the meatballs breaking up during Balti-ing.

Remove them carefully with a slotted spoon and set aside, keeping 2 ladles of the stock from the saucepan for use in the Balti.

Stage 3: Balti method

Heat the ghee or oil in a large wok over a moderately high heat and fry the remaining chopped onions until they are just turning brown. Add the ginger, garlic, green pepper and remaining green chillies. Stir violently and add the reserved stock from the meatballs.

Put in the rest of the salt, methi, chopped coriander and garam masala. Stir everything together and add the tomato purée and tomatoes. Sprinkle the remaining cumin seeds over the top and stir-fry for 5 minutes.

Lower the meatballs into the mixture and cook, stirring gently, for 10 more minutes.

Divide the meatballs among 4 warmed Balti bowls, pour the sauce over each one and serve.

YASSER'S LAMB DHANSAK BALTI
(Proprietor Mr S. Khan, Chef Mr Shokat Ali)

'Dhansak' is a sweet and sour dish with lentils. There is a nutty hint to the taste of lamb that works so well in unison with the lentils. This is a delicious Balti, suitable for a dinner party or a family meal, although not for very young children.

3 Stages • Fairly spicy • Serves 4

*900 g / 2 lb lamb, cut into 2.5 cm / 1 inch
    cubes and par-cooked (using
    ingredients from page 22)*
115 g / 4 oz yellow split peas
8 tbsp vegetable ghee or oil
1 tbsp garlic powder

1 tbsp dried methi
5 ladles of Balti sauce
3 tbsp chopped fresh coriander
1/2 tsp garam masala (page 25)
2 tomatoes, each cut into 8 pieces

Stage 1: Par-cooking the lamb and making the Balti sauce
See page 22.

Stage 2: Pre-cooking the split peas
See page 24.

Stage 3: Balti method
Heat the ghee or oil in a large wok over a moderate flame. Stir in the garlic powder and methi, and pour in 4 ladles of Balti sauce. Add the coriander and lamb. Put in the lentils (they're called 'dal' now that they're cooked). Add more Balti sauce, the garam masala and pieces of tomato.

Turn the heat down to low, stir carefully once and cook for 7 minutes. By this time the Balti should have dried out quite a lot. If it is still not dry enough turn the heat up again to reduce the mixture.

Divide among 4 warmed Balti bowls and serve.

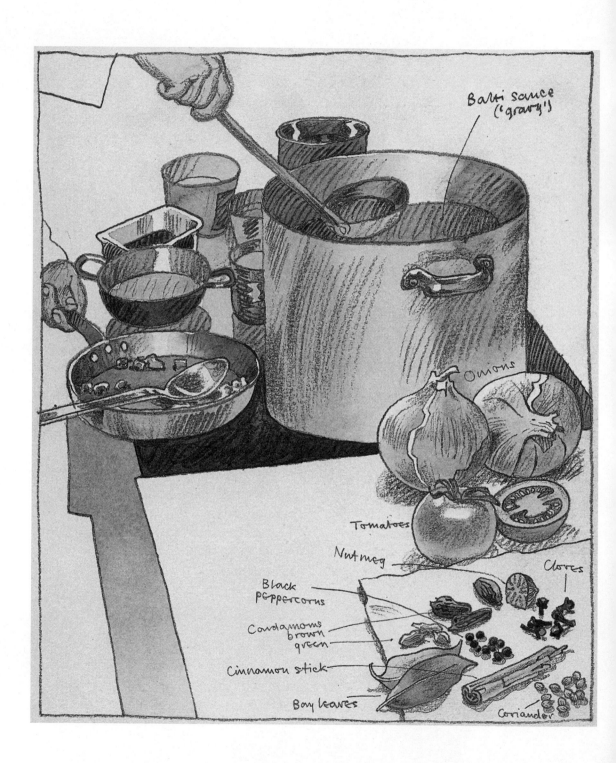

Balti sauce ('gravy')

Onions

Tomatoes

Nutmeg

Cloves

Black peppercorns

Cardamoms
brown
green

Cinnamon stick

Bay leaves

Coriander

FISH AND SHELLFISH BALTIS

AKASH'S PRAWN AND BHINDI (LADIES' FINGERS) BALTI

(Proprietor M. Abdul Kadir, Chefs M. Abdul and A. Nesar)

If 'Jack Woolley' hadn't left Stirchley for Ambridge this would have been his local Baltihouse! Ladies' fingers have a lovely sticky, 'beany' taste that contrasts well with the sea-flavour of prawns. This recipe uses a special, richly flavoured Balti paste. Despite its many stages, it's well worth the effort.

5 Stages • Medium • A dinner party dish • Serves 4

450 g / 1 lb peeled cooked prawns
450 g / 1 lb ladies' fingers (okra), topped-and-tailed
170 g / 6 oz yellow split peas
70 g / 2 1/2 oz butter
4 cm / 1 1/2 inch cube fresh ginger, peeled and grated
14 large garlic cloves, crushed
4 large onions, chopped
1 carrot, sliced
4 tbsp chopped fresh coriander, stems as

well as leaves, plus a little extra to garnish
1 green pepper, seeded and chopped
4 tomatoes, 3 chopped, 1 sliced
1 tbsp tomato purée
2 tbsp dried methi
5 tsp Balti spice mix (page 26)
1 tsp curry powder
2 tsp turmeric powder
2 tsp garam masala (page 25)
6 tbsp vegetable oil
6-7 ladles of Balti sauce

Stage 1: Making the Balti sauce
See page 24.

Stage 2: Pre-cooking the split peas
See page 24.

Stage 3: Par-cooking the ladies' fingers
See page 23.

Stage 4: Making Akash's Balti paste
Heat the butter in a saucepan over a moderate flame and fry half the ginger, half the garlic, and half the chopped onions. When the onions are becoming translucent add the carrot, chopped coriander, half the green pepper, chopped tomatoes, tomato purée and the pre-cooked split peas. Stir-fry for 2 minutes.

Remove from the heat. When cool enough to handle spoon into a blender or food processor and liquidise. If you have to, moisten with a little water. Stir in the methi, spice mix, curry powder, turmeric and garam masala. You should have a thick paste.

Stage 5: Balti method

Heat the oil in a large wok over moderately high heat. Fry the rest of the ginger and garlic for 3 minutes. Put in the prawns and the remaining green peppers and chopped onions. Stir-fry for 2 minutes. Add 4 ladles of the Akash Balti paste. Make sure that this is well integrated before putting in the ladies' fingers. Moisten everything with 6 ladles of Balti sauce, keeping the rest for final adjustments.

Shake and stir, like a professional Balti chef, for a further 3 minutes. (Catching the Balti alight as Mr Nesar did is not obligatory. This is a regular part of Baltihouse kitchen drama, and they merely shake the flames out!)

Divide among 4 warmed Balti bowls, putting 2 small slices of tomato on each. Garnish further with a little chopped coriander and serve.

AL MOUGHAL'S BALTI FISH
(Proprietor and Chef Mr Moughal)

Marinading the fish for ¹/₂ hour, then making a simple Balti sauce are two of the stages in this Balti. The fish is then cooked in the wok – no need for par-cooking. An uncomplicated dish with few spices, allowing the flavour of the fish to come through. Because hake doesn't have small bones, children as well as adults will go a bundle on it.

3 Stages • Mild • Serves 4

900 g / 2 lb silver hake, skinned and filleted
2 tsp Balti spice mix (page 26)
¹/₂ tsp turmeric powder
300 ml / ¹/₂ pint plain yoghurt
3 tbsp vegetable oil
2 onions, chopped
2 tsp ground coriander
2 tsp garam masala (page 25)

1 tsp chilli powder
2 tomatoes, chopped
4 cm / 1¹/₂ inch cube fresh ginger, peeled and grated
6 large garlic cloves, crushed
4-6 ladles of Balti sauce
1 tbsp chopped fresh coriander
1 tsp dried methi

Stage 1: Marinading the fish
Removing the bones from hake is very easy to do. There is really only the one large cross-shaped bone running through the middle, and few small bones to watch out for.

Cut or flake the fish into small pieces and lay them in a large dish. Sprinkle them with the Balti spice mix and turmeric and spoon the yoghurt over them. Toss the pieces well to ensure they are evenly covered. Put to one side to marinade for 30 minutes.

Stage 2: Making the Balti sauce
See page 24.

Stage 3: Balti method
Heat the oil in a large wok over a moderate flame. Fry the onions until they are soft but not turning brown. In quick succession put in the ground coriander, garam masala, chilli powder, tomatoes, ginger and garlic, stirring when you can amongst all this activity! Allow to cook for a couple of minutes still on moderate heat, then add the flaked fish and its marinade. Stir well and let this cook for another 3-4 minutes.

Cover with 4 ladles of Balti sauce, and add the fresh coriander and the dried methi. Mix well. Turn the heat to low and simmer for 4 minutes. Add more Balti sauce if the mixture is too dry.

Divide among 4 warmed Balti dishes and serve with plain naan or chapatis.

BALTI BAZAAR'S PRAWN PATHIAWALA BALTI
(Partners Mohammed Abdul Kadir and Rokib Ali who is also Chef)

Mr Ali loves cooking. This Balti is evidence in itself. It cleverly balances the spices, the prawns and a subtle mix of fruit and cream!

2 Stages • Mild • A dinner party dish that is simple enough to cook for the family • Serves 4

450 g / 1 lb peeled large prawns, cooked
   and squeezed of most of their liquid
8 tbsp vegetable ghee or oil
12 garlic cloves, crushed
5 tsp Balti spice mix (page 26)
1 tbsp garam masala (page 25)
6 ladles of Balti sauce
2.5 cm / 1 inch cinnamon stick
2 brown cardamoms, broken slightly open
6 whole cloves

1/2 tsp ground fennel
2 tsp dried methi
1/2 tsp lovage seeds (ajwan), optional
2 tsp salt
8 large grapes, seeded if necessary
1 apple, cored and sliced
1 pear, cored and sliced
1 tomato, chopped
3 tbsp single cream

Stage 1: Making the Balti sauce
See page 24.

Stage 2: Balti method
Heat the ghee or oil in a large wok over moderately high heat. Stir-fry the garlic for a few seconds, then quickly stir in the spice mix and garam masala. Put in the Balti sauce, cinnamon stick, cardamoms, cloves, fennel, methi, lovage, salt and the fruit.

Pat the prawns dry on kitchen paper. Stir them in and cook for 3-5 minutes, drying the mixture off a little. Turn the heat to low and add the tomato and 4 teaspoons of cream. Stir for about half a minute and then remove from the heat.

Divide among 4 warmed Balti bowls and garnish each with a trickle of cream.

N.B. If you are using frozen prawns the temptation will be to put them in before they are completely defrosted. If you do they will release a lot of liquid into the Balti and you will have to reduce the mixture for perhaps another 5 minutes.

BHANGRA BEAT'S INDUS VALLEY BALTI TROUT
(Partners Mr Kabir and Mr Shamim, Chef Mr Sadiqur Choudhury)

A delicious fish dish. The mild spices don't hide the delicate flavour of the trout. You could serve this as a starter if you halve the quantities.

2 Stages • Medium spiced • Serves 4

4 trout, cleaned, rinsed and patted dry
plain flour
8 tbsp vegetable oil
1 tbsp chopped fresh coriander
2 fresh green chillies, whole
2 dried red chillies, whole
2 onions, finely sliced

2.5 cm / 1 inch cube fresh ginger, peeled
*   and grated*
4 large garlic cloves, crushed
4 tsp tomato purée
1/2 tsp chilli powder
2 1/2 tsp turmeric powder
1 tsp salt

Stage 1: Par-cooking the trout

Dust the trout liberally with flour. Heat a little of the oil in a large wok on moderate heat and fry the trout for 2 minutes on each side. Take them out and set aside.

In the oil remaining in the wok fry the chopped coriander and both sorts of chilli for 2 more minutes. Take them out with a slotted spoon and set aside too.

Stage 2: Balti method

Add the remaining oil to the wok and fry the onions, ginger and garlic over high heat until the onions begin to change colour. Add the tomato purée, chilli powder and turmeric. Stir them in well and

then add the salt and 300 ml / 1/2 pint water. Cover the wok with a lid and bring to the boil. Cook, covered, for 5 minutes. Turn the heat to moderate and cook, still covered and stirring from time to time, for 15 more minutes.

Now add the trout, coriander and chillies. Stir, making sure the fish are well covered in sauce. Be gentle; the fish shouldn't break. Replace the lid, turn the heat to low and cook for a further 20 minutes, undisturbed.

Remove from the heat and let the Balti rest for 10 minutes with the lid still on. Heat through quickly just before dividing among 4 warmed Balti bowls and serving.

CELEBRITY'S SCAMPI BALTI
(Partner Mr Aziz, Chef Dinesh Dhingra)

The fish taste comes through strongly and the cream smooths the corners of the spices, making for a delicious dish. It has quite a liquid sauce.

2 Stages • Mild • A very simple Balti, definitely for a dinner party • Serves 4

340-450 g / ¾-1 lb shelled scampi
8 tbsp vegetable oil
4 cm / 1 ½ inch cube fresh ginger, peeled
    and grated
6 garlic cloves, crushed

1 fresh green chilli, very finely chopped
1 tsp salt
8 ladles of Balti sauce
1 ½ tbsp garam masala (page 25)
1 tbsp chopped fresh coriander

Stage 1: Making the Balti sauce
See page 24.

Stage 2: Balti method
Rinse the scampi under running water and pat dry on kitchen paper. Heat the oil in a large wok over moderate heat and fry the ginger and garlic until golden brown. Add the green chilli and the scampi. Stir well and then add the salt, 6 ladles of the

Balti sauce, garam masala and chopped coriander. Cook for about 6 minutes on a high heat, stirring all the time. Add the remaining 2 ladles of sauce, reduce the heat and cook for another 6 minutes. If there is a little oil on the surface spoon it off.

Divide among 4 warmed Balti bowls and serve.

CHANNI'S KING PRAWN JALFREZI BALTI
(Proprietor and Chef Mr 'Channi' Dogra)

A beautifully spiced dish with a touch of tomato-ey sweetness, complementing the subtle sea taste of the king prawns. This is quite a dry dish. Channi likes it like this way (and so do we) but, he says, many of his clients prefer it moister. You can easily achieve this by adding some Balti sauce (page 24).

1 Stage • Medium hot • A dinner party or special occasion dish • Serves 4

20 raw king prawns, peeled and washed

3 tbsp vegetable ghee or oil

3 onions, 2 1/2 sliced longways and 1/2 chopped

2.5 cm / 1 inch cube fresh ginger, peeled and grated

3 garlic cloves, crushed

1 tsp cumin seeds

1/2 tsp salt

1 tbsp tomato purée

2 tsp ground cumin

2 tsp ground coriander

2 tomatoes, chopped

1 fresh green chilli, ground in a mortar or very finely chopped

1/2 green pepper, seeded and cut into 5 mm / 1/4 inch strips

1/2 red pepper, seeded and cut into 5 mm / 1/4 inch strips

1 tbsp chopped fresh coriander

Heat 2 tablespoons of the vegetable ghee or oil in a large wok. Add the onions that have been sliced longways and fry on a low heat until soft and translucent. Add the grated ginger and crushed garlic to the onions. Now, in quick succession, cooking over a moderately high heat and stirring all the time, sprinkle in the whole cumin seeds, salt, tomato purée, ground cumin and ground coriander. The mixture will get rather dry at this point, so add half of the chopped tomatoes to moisten it.

Now put in the green chilli, the remaining vegetable ghee or oil and then the prawns, continuing to stir all the time. Put in the onion that has been chopped. This means the finished dish will have some well-done onion in it as well as some with a little of its natural raw crunchiness left. This is typical of the subtlety of Channi's recipes.

Stir in the rest of the chopped tomato. Add the strips of peppers and the chopped coriander to the wok. Stir. Remove from the heat after a couple of minutes so the peppers retain some of their crispness.

Divide among 4 warmed Balti bowls and serve.

KHANUM'S PRAWN MADRAS BALTI
(Proprietors Diana and Derek, Chef Mr Ali)

This Balti has the fiery Madras chilli-ness which somehow does not overwhelm the delicate flavour of the prawns. Make sure your dinner guests like spicy food.

2 Stages • Very hot • Serves 4

450 g / 1 lb peeled cooked prawns
7 tbsp vegetable oil
4 cm / 1 1/2 inch cube fresh ginger, peeled
*   and grated*
6 large garlic cloves
2 onions, chopped
1 green pepper, seeded and diced
2 tomatoes, chopped

salt to taste
5 tsp Balti spice mix (page 26)
2 tsp lemon juice
4 tsp chilli powder (halve this amount if
*   you prefer)*
2 heaped tsp tomato purée
7-8 ladles of Balti sauce
2 tsp chopped fresh coriander to garnish

Stage 1: Making the Balti sauce
See page 24.

Stage 2: Balti method
Heat the oil in a large wok over moderately high heat and stir-fry the ginger and garlic for 1 minute. Put in the onions and fry until they are just turning brown. Add the green pepper, tomatoes and 3/4 teaspoon of salt. Stir and shake for 2 minutes, then add the Balti spice mix. Stir in the prawns, lemon juice, chilli powder, tomato purée and 7 ladles of Balti sauce. Cook, stirring all the time, for 3 minutes. Adjust the consistency by reducing the mixture or adding more Balti sauce. Adjust the seasoning.

Divide among 4 warmed Balti bowls and serve garnished with chopped coriander.

KHYBER PASS' PRAWN, MUSHROOM, SPINACH AND CHICK PEA BALTI

(Chef Mr Shabir)

The prawns go so well with the vegetables in this Balti. The mushrooms, spinach and green chillies make a soft dark green contrast to the slight crunch of the chick peas and prawns.

3 Stages • Medium hot • A special family meal or party dish • Serves

340 g / 3/4 lb small peeled cooked prawns
115 g / 1/4 lb mushrooms, sliced
450 g / 1 lb fresh spinach, cooked, drained
and chopped, or use 200 g / 7 oz frozen
spinach, thawed and drained
140 g / 5 oz dried chick peas, or use a
300 g / 10 oz can, drained
8 tbsp vegetable ghee or oil
1 onion, chopped

2 fresh green chillies, finely chopped
1 tbsp garlic powder
2 tomatoes, thickly sliced
1/2 tsp chilli powder
2-3 tsp salt
4-5 ladles of Balti sauce
2 tbsp chopped fresh coriander
2 tbsp dried methi, stalks picked out,
rubbed between your hands

Stage 1: Pre-cooking the chick peas
See page 24. Or open the can and drain well.

Stage 2: Making the Balti sauce
See page 24.

Stage 3: Balti method
Heat the ghee or oil in a large wok over moderate heat and fry the onion until it is turning brown. Add in quick succession,

stirring when you can, the prawns, chopped chillies, garlic powder, tomatoes and chilli powder. Stir in the mushrooms, spinach, chick peas and salt to taste. Cook, stirring gently all the time, for 2 minutes.

Add 4 ladles of the Balti sauce, the fresh coriander and methi and cook, still stirring, for 3 minutes longer. Add more Balti sauce if the mixture is too dry.

Divide among 4 warmed Balti bowls and serve with naan bread.

MEMSAHIB'S OYSTER BALTI

(Proprietors Mr and Mrs A. and S. O'Flaherty, Chef Mr Yassim)

The oysters become part of the overall flavour. It is, interestingly, echoed by the taste of fresh coriander. The recipe uses frozen oysters, but you can, of course, use fresh ones.

2 Stages • Mild • For a special occasion • Serves 4

20 shelled oysters
8 tbsp vegetable oil
4 tomatoes, quartered
3 tbsp chopped fresh coriander

2 tbsp garlic powder
8 ladles of Balti sauce
1 1/2 tbsp dried methi
1 tsp garam masala (page 25)

Stage 1: Making the Balti sauce
See page 24.

Stage 2: Balti method
Heat the oil in a large wok over moderately high heat. Fry the tomatoes, breaking them up with the spoon. Add the fresh coriander and garlic powder. Sear them for about a minute, then add the Balti sauce. Stir well and put in the methi and oysters. Cook, stirring all the time, for 2 minutes.

Divide among 4 warmed Balti bowls and serve aromatised with a sprinkle of garam masala. Eat with chapatis.

MUSSELS BALTI

(Chefs Diane Lowe and Mike Davidson)

Our own recipe takes fresh mussels cooked in white wine to create an exotic Balti with a gently spiced sauce.

3 Stages • Mild • A special occasion dinner • Serves 4

900 g / 2 lb fresh mussels, cleaned
25 g / 1 oz butter
2 onions, finely chopped
1 garlic clove, crushed
300 ml / 1/2 pint dry white wine
1 tbsp chopped parsley
3 tbsp chopped fresh coriander
freshly ground black pepper
8 tbsp vegetable oil or ghee
2 fresh green chillies, finely chopped

2 tomatoes, thickly sliced
3 ladles of Balti sauce
1 tbsp garlic powder
1/2 tsp chilli powder
1 tsp salt
2 tbsp dried methi, rubbed between your
   hands
1 tbsp single cream
garam masala to garnish (page 25)

Stage 1: Making the Balti sauce

See page 24.

Stage 2: Cooking the mussels

Melt the butter in a large saucepan. Put in 1 of the onions, the crushed garlic, wine, parsley and 1 tablespoon of chopped coriander. Add the mussels and cover with a lid. Shake the pan over a high heat for 3-5 minutes or until the shells are open.

Take the mussels out, discarding any that haven't opened. Strain the liquid and reserve 115 ml / 4 floz. Remove the mussels from their shells and sprinkle them with plenty of ground black pepper.

Stage 3: Balti method

Heat the oil or ghee in a large wok over a moderate heat and fry the remaining

chopped onion until it is just turning colour. Add the chillies and the tomatoes, breaking them up with the edge of the spoon as you stir. Next add the Balti sauce and bring to the boil. In quick succession add the garlic powder, chilli powder, salt, methi and remaining chopped coriander. Add the reserved mussel cooking liquid. Cook, stirring, on a moderate heat for about 5 minutes. If the sauce becomes too dry add small amounts of water.

Stir in the cream, a little at a time. Finally add the mussels. Cook for a very short time, just long enough to heat them through.

Divide among 4 warmed Balti bowls and serve, garnishing each with a pinch of garam masala.

PANJAB TANDOORI'S KING PRAWN BALTI
(Proprietor and Chef Kailash Watts)

A luxurious, rich Balti. An important part of it is Mr Watts' own tomato purée, which includes fresh basil.

3 Stages • Mild • A dinner party recipe • Serves 4

340 g / ³/₄ lb raw king prawns, peeled and
    black thread removed
¹/₂ tsp chopped fresh basil
2 tsp chopped fresh mint
200 g / 7 oz butter
¹/₂ tsp freshly ground black pepper
450 g / 1 lb fresh tomatoes, peeled, or use
    canned, plus 2 small tomatoes,
    chopped, for the Balti stage
3 onions, chopped
¹/₂ green pepper, seeded and diced

¹/₂-³/₄ tsp salt
5 cm / 2 inch cube fresh ginger, peeled
    and grated
10 garlic cloves, crushed
3 ladles of Balti sauce
3 palmfuls of dried methi
2 fresh green chillies, seeded and finely
    chopped
3 tbsp chopped fresh coriander
115 ml / 4 fl oz single cream
2 tsp garam masala (page 25)

Stage 1: Making the Balti sauce
See page 24.

Stage 2: Making the tomato purée
Melt 15 g / ¹/₂ oz of the butter in a heavy saucepan and fry the basil and mint for half a minute. Add the black pepper, peeled tomatoes and salt. Reduce the mixture by cooking gently for about 30 minutes. Chop the tomatoes with the spoon as you cook them. Remove from the heat and keep ready for the Balti.

Stage 3: Balti method
Heat the rest of the butter in a large wok over moderately high heat. Stir-fry the onions and green pepper for about 5 minutes. Add the ginger, garlic, Balti sauce, 3 ladles of Mr Watts' tomato purée, the methi and green chillies. Stir everything well.

Put in the king prawns and stir them around. Add the chopped coriander, saving a little for the garnish, the chopped tomato, the cream, saving a little of that too, and the garam masala. Stir-fry for 5 minutes.

Divide among 4 warmed Balti bowls and serve garnished with a sprinkle of chopped coriander and a dribble of cream.

PREET PALACE'S PRAWN PATHIA BALTI
(Proprietor Mr Mittel, Chef Mr Sajjad)

Particularly popular with Diane, this Balti is hot and sour and sweet and delicious. Because it is so simple, it can be a family treat.

3 Stages • Medium hot • Suitable for entertaining • Serves 4

340 g / 3/4 lb small peeled cooked prawns
170 g / 6 oz yellow split peas, or use a
    400 g / 14 oz can
2 tsp turmeric powder
3 tsp salt
6 tbsp vegetable oil
2 cm / 3/4 inch cube fresh ginger, peeled
    and grated
2 large garlic cloves, crushed

1 tsp chilli powder
1 1/2 tbsp sugar
5 tsp Balti spice mix (page 26)
1 tbsp tomato purée
4 tbsp lemon juice
1 green pepper, seeded and chopped
2 large handfuls of chopped fresh
    coriander
4 ladles of Balti sauce

Stage 1: Pre-cooking the split peas
Cook the split peas with 1 teaspoon of the turmeric powder, 1 teaspoon of the salt and 600 ml / 1 pint water (see page 24). Or open the can and drain well.

Stage 2: Making the Balti sauce
See page 24.

Stage 3: Balti method
Have all the ingredients weighed and measured handy to the stove so you can move very fast.

Heat the oil in a large wok over moderate heat and fry the ginger and garlic for 30 seconds. Now add the prawns and 1 teaspoon of the salt. Stir them around and, in quick succession, add all the other ingredients, including the remaining turmeric.

Turn the heat to high and stir and shake for 3 minutes. You might have to reduce the sauce a little. Check to see if you need to add more salt, and cook for 1 more minute.

About 6-7 minutes of slightly frantic work and you have a delicious meal! Divide among 4 warmed Balti bowls and serve.

ROYAL NAIM'S FISH MASALA BALTI
(Proprietor Mr Azim, Chef Mohammad Nazir)

In terms of flavour this is a dish where the pieces of fish retain their individuality in a sea of spicy sauce. It surprises us how quite subtle tastes can hold their own in robust company, as the fish does here. It is probably not a dish for children or beginners, but would make an ideal dinner party dish for spice lovers.

2 Stages • Fairly hot • Serves 4

570 g / 1¹/₄ lb silver hake, skinned and
    filleted
3 tbsp vegetable ghee or oil
4 cm / 1¹/₂ inch cube fresh ginger, peeled
    and grated
4 garlic cloves, crushed
¹/₂ green pepper, seeded and chopped
2-3 fresh green chillies, finely chopped

1¹/₂ palmfuls of chopped fresh coriander,
    plus a few leaves to garnish
8 ladles of Balti sauce
2 tsp garam masala (page 25)
2 tsp dried methi
150 ml / ¹/₄ pint plain yoghurt
1-2 tbsp red food colouring (optional)

Stage 1: Making the Balti sauce
See page 24.

Stage 2: Balti method
Heat the ghee or oil in a large wok over high heat and fry the ginger, garlic and green pepper until the pepper is soft. Stir in the chillies and coriander and fry for 2 minutes. Add the pieces of fish and the Balti sauce and stir-fry for 3 more minutes.

Now put in the garam masala and dried methi.

Stir the yoghurt, with or without the food colouring, into the mixture in the wok ¹/₂ tablespoon at a time. Cook gently for another minute.

Divide among 4 warmed Balti bowls and garnish each with a couple of leaves of fresh coriander. The green will contrast beautifully with the terracotta colour of the food.

SPICE VALLEY'S TIGER PRAWN SPECIAL BALTI

(Proprietor Mr Alom, Chef Nazir Ahmed)

The sharp intake of breath of the brandy, then the strong flavour of king prawns and the tingling on the lips of the spices! Wonderful! A luxury Balti – spicy, but not too hot..

3 Stages • Spicy • A special occasion Balti • Serves 4

16 large raw tiger prawns, peeled
8 tbsp vegetable oil
3 onions, chopped
1/2 green pepper, seeded and diced
4 tomatoes, thinly sliced
5 tsp Balti spice mix (page 26)
2 tsp chilli powder

2 tsp garam masala (page 25)
1 1/2 tbsp tomato purée
2 tbsp dried methi
2 tbsp chopped fresh coriander
8 ladles of Balti sauce
4 tbsp white wine
3 tbsp brandy

Stage 1: Making the Balti sauce
See page 24.

Stage 2: Preparing the prawns
Split the tiger prawns down the back and remove the black thread. Cut each one into three pieces. Rinse them, gently squeeze out excess water and pat them dry on kitchen paper.

Stage 3: Balti method
Heat the oil in a large wok over low heat and put in the tiger prawns. Add the onions and green pepper and fry until the onions are soft and translucent. Add the tomatoes, Balti spice mix, chilli powder, garam masala, tomato purée, methi, chopped coriander and the Balti sauce. Pour in the wine and stir well, breaking up the tomatoes as you do. Cook, still stirring, for 3 more minutes.

Pour the brandy over and set alight. Turn the heat up to reduce the sauce.

Divide among 4 warmed Balti bowls and serve.

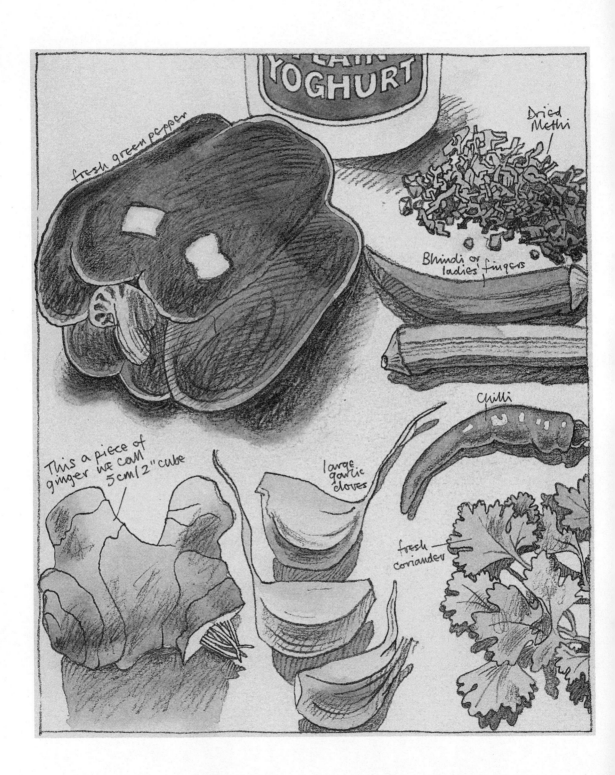

VEGETABLE BALTIS

BALTI SOCIETY'S TINDA BALTI
(Proprietor Mr Hanif, Chef Mr R. Dhingra)

Mr Hanif has a different theory as to why the bowl is called a 'balti'. He says that the dish called 'Karahi' was banned as being too wasteful so shopkeepers merely re-named it 'bucket' or 'balti' and it kept that name when it arrived in Birmingham. Tinda is a Punjabi vegetable unobtainable except in specialist Asian shops. It is subtle in flavour and we love it in Baltis.

2 Stages • Mild • Vegetarian • Serves 4

12 fresh tinda, roughly chopped, or use canned
6 tbsp vegetable oil
2.5 cm / 1 inch cube fresh ginger, peeled and grated
6 garlic cloves, crushed

2 tomatoes, chopped
1/2 tsp chilli powder
8 ladles of Balti sauce
1 tbsp chopped fresh coriander
2 tbsp double cream

Stage 1: Making the Balti sauce
See page 24.

Stage 2: Balti method
Heat the oil in a large wok over a moderate flame. Stir-fry the ginger, garlic and tomatoes for 1 minute or until reduced to a pulp. Add the tinda and stir-fry violently for 2 minutes.

Add 7 ladles of the Balti sauce, keeping the rest to adjust the moisture later. Turn the heat down and cook at a fast simmer for 3 more minutes. Add the chopped coriander and cream. Stir in well and serve in warmed Balti bowls.

CELEBRITY'S SWEETCORN AND POTATO BALTI
(Partner Mr Aziz, Chef Dinesh Dhingra)

A simple vegetarian Balti, this has a pleasing orangey sauce with yellow spots of corn.

3 Stages • Peppery hot • Ideal for the family • Serves 4

2 x 395 g / 14 oz cans sweetcorn, drained
450 g / 1 lb potatoes
6 tbsp vegetable oil
4 cm / 1¹/₂ inch cube fresh ginger, peeled and grated
6 large garlic cloves, crushed

2 fresh green chillies, very finely chopped
1 tsp salt
8 ladles of Balti sauce
1¹/₂ tbsp garam masala (page 25)
1 tbsp chopped fresh coriander

Stage 1: Making the Balti sauce
See page 24.

Stage 2: Par-cooking the potatoes
Cook the potatoes in boiling salted water until just starting to be tender. Drain and let them cool. Cut them into bite-size pieces.

Stage 3: Balti method
Heat the oil in a large wok over a moderate flame. Fry the potatoes for 3-4 minutes. Add the ginger and garlic and fry until turning brown. Add the chillies, sweetcorn, salt and Balti sauce. Stir well and then add the garam masala and coriander. Cook for 5-6 minutes or until the potatoes and corn are heated through.

Divide among 4 warmed Balti bowls and serve.

FAISAL SUNDOWN'S BLACK EYE BEAN AND MUSHROOM BALTI
(Proprietor and Chef Mr Affar)

This is a rich, dark and healthy dish. The taste of the beans works extremely well with the mushrooms. With a simple naan, or a garlic one if you prefer, it makes a meal on its own.

3 Stages • Medium spiced • Ideal for a family meal • Serves 4

400 g / 14 oz dried black eye beans, or use
   canned beans
170 g / 6 oz button mushrooms, finely
   chopped
6 tbsp vegetable oil
8 garlic cloves, crushed
3 tomatoes, roughly chopped

1/2 fresh green chilli, very finely chopped
2 palmfuls of chopped fresh coriander
1 tbsp tomato purée
2 1/2 tsp Balti spice mix (page 26)
1/2 tsp turmeric powder
3/4 tsp salt
4-6 ladles of Balti sauce

Stage 1: Pre-cooking the beans
See page 24. Or open the can of beans and drain well.

Stage 2: Making the Balti sauce
See page 24.

Stage 3: Balti method
Put the oil into a large wok and turn the heat up quite high. Add the crushed garlic and fry for a minute before you put in the tomatoes, green chilli and the fresh coriander. Stir-fry for 2 more minutes.

Add the tomato purée, spice mix, turmeric and 1/2 teaspoon of the salt.

Now add 4 ladles of the Balti sauce and stir it around to incorporate all the spice mixture. Turn the heat down to moderate and add the drained black eye beans and the mushrooms. Stir-fry, gently shaking the wok, until the beans are done (test by bite!). This will take about 5 minutes. Adjust the seasoning with the remaining salt, and add more sauce if the mixture is too dry.

Divide among 4 warmed Balti bowls and serve with naan bread or chapatis.

HIGH QUALITY BALTI'S GHOBI, PALAK AND CHANA (CAULIFLOWER, SPINACH AND CHICK PEA) BALTI
(Proprietor and Chef Mr Begg)

A vegetarian Balti combining the flavour of brassicas with the nutty taste of chick peas. Because you add the chillies towards the end of the cooking they retain their fresh sharpness too. This is suitable for a dinner party or a family meal with older children.

3 Stages • Quite hot • Serves 4

340 g / ³/4 lb cauliflower, broken into
    small florets
570 g / 1¹/4 lb fresh spinach, cooked and
    drained, or use 400 g / 14 oz frozen
    spinach, thawed and drained
425 g / 15 oz dried chick peas, or use
    canned
5 tbsp vegetable oil
4 onions, chopped

2.5 cm / 1 inch cube fresh ginger, peeled
    and grated
6 garlic cloves, crushed
2 tsp salt
4 tomatoes, chopped
4-6 ladles of Balti sauce
2-3 fresh green chillies, finely chopped
1 tbsp chopped fresh coriander
1 tsp garam masala (page 25)

Stage 1: Pre-cooking the chick peas
See page 24. Or open the can and drain well.

Stage 2: Making the Balti sauce
See page 24.

Stage 3: Balti method
Heat the oil in a large wok and fry the onions gently until they are just turning brown. Add the ginger and garlic and stir well. Let them 'cook-in' for a couple of minutes before you put in the spinach and the salt. Add the tomatoes, cauliflower florets, chick peas and 4 ladles of Balti sauce and stir all the ingredients well together, making sure that all the vegetables are covered in sauce. Add up to another 2 ladles of Balti sauce, a little at a time, if the mixture is too dry.

Turn the heat to low, cover with a lid and simmer until the cauliflower is just tender but retains its bite.

Add the green chillies and stir-fry for 3 more minutes. Adding the chillies at this late stage preserves a lot of their heat, and keeps their flavour as a separate high-note.

Divide among 4 warmed Balti dishes and garnish each one with chopped coriander and garam masala. Serve with chapati (we like the wholewheat taste with this dish) or naan bread.

ISTAFA'S MUSTARD LEAF (OR SPINACH AND MUSTARD) BALTI

(Proprietor Mrs Shaheen Sultana, Chef Mr Moor Ahmed)

Fresh mustard leaf is available only from Asian shops, and then only in season. Instead this dish can be made using spinach and English mustard. Several of the Balti chefs, including Mr Ahmed, have said 'no ginger in vegetable dishes'. This is a case in point. Serve as an unusual vegetarian Balti main course, or as an accompaniment to another main course Balti.

2 Stages • Mild • Serves 4

450 g / 1 lb mustard leaf, washed,
  de-stalked and chopped, or use 450 g /
  1 lb spinach, washed, de-stalked and
  chopped, and 1 tsp made English
  mustard
6 tbsp vegetable ghee or oil
2 onions, chopped

6 garlic cloves, crushed
1/2 tsp salt
4 ladles of Balti sauce
1 tbsp Balti spice mix (page 26)
1 tsp turmeric powder
2 tbsp chopped fresh coriander
1 1/2 tbsp dried methi

Stage 1: Making the Balti sauce
Make Istafa's on page 54, or see page 24.

Stage 2: Balti method
Put the ghee or oil into a large wok and heat it over a moderate flame. Fry the onions and garlic with a touch of salt for a few minutes. Drop in the mustard leaf, or spinach, and cover with Balti sauce. Stir well and turn the heat to low. Cook for 5 minutes.

Sprinkle in the spice mix, turmeric, coriander and methi. Add the mustard if you are using spinach. Cover the wok and simmer for about 10 minutes.

Take the lid off. If the dish is too moist reduce by turning the heat up. Taste and adjust the salt and, if you're cooking with spinach, the mustard.

Divide among 4 warmed Balti bowls and serve.

KHAN'S CHICK PEA AND MUSHROOM BHUNA BALTI

(Proprietor Mr Khan, Chef Mr Khan (another one!))

A simple vegetarian dish that does, however, involve soaking the chick peas overnight (or cheat and use canned chick peas!). This is a dish with very little sauce: 'bhuna' means a dry dish.

2 Stages • Medium • Serves 4

*285 g / 10 oz dried chick peas, or use
  1 large can*
170 g / 6 oz button mushrooms, sliced
6 tbsp vegetable oil
2 onions, chopped
1 fresh green chilli, chopped
3 tomatoes, roughly chopped

1 tsp curry powder
1 tsp turmeric powder
1/2 tsp ground coriander
*1/2 tsp garam masala, plus a little extra
  to garnish (page 25)*
11/2-2 tsp salt

Stage 1: Pre-cooking the chick peas

See page 24; after draining, reserve 150 ml/ 1/4 pint of the cooking liquid. Or open the can and drain, reserving the required quantity of liquid.

Stage 2: Balti method

Heat the oil in a large wok on moderate heat and fry the onions until they are starting to turn brown. Add the chopped chilli and tomatoes and cook, stirring, for 3 minutes or until the tomatoes are beginning to break up and the chilli is getting soft.

Stir in the chick peas with the reserved cooking liquid and the curry powder, turmeric, ground coriander and garam masala. Bring to the boil. Turn the heat down and simmer, stirring, for 5 minutes.

Add the sliced mushrooms and salt to taste and shake and stir for a further 2 minutes.

Divide among 4 warmed Balti bowls and serve, sprinkling each with an extra pinch of garam masala.

KHYBER'S POTATO, MUSHROOM AND GREEN PEPPER BALTI

(Proprietor Mr Sarwar, Chefs Mrs Sarwar and Mr A. Rais)

In this Balti, the peppers retain some of their crunch, the potatoes have a 'cosiness' of taste and there is a soft earthiness to the mushrooms.

3 Stages • Mild • A delicious vegetarian Balti • Serves 4

450 g / 1 lb potatoes, peeled
340 g / 3/4 lb mushrooms, sliced
2 large green peppers, seeded and thinly
    sliced
10 tbsp vegetable oil
1 tsp cumin seeds
2 onions, chopped

4 cm / 1 1/2 inch cube fresh ginger, peeled
    and grated
6 garlic cloves, crushed
1/2 tsp chilli powder
1/2 tsp salt
600 ml / 1 pint Balti sauce
1 heaped tsp garam masala (page 25)
2 tbsp chopped fresh coriander

Stage 1: Making the Balti sauce
See page 24.

Stage 2: Pre-cooking the potatoes
Cook the potatoes in boiling salted water until just tender; drain. When they are cool enough to handle cut them into 2 cm / 3/4 inch cubes.

Heat 4 tablespoons of the oil in a frying pan over moderate heat. Put in the cumin seeds. After a few seconds add the chopped onions and fry them until they become translucent. Put in the potatoes and fry gently for 5 minutes, stirring occasionally. Remove from the heat and take the potatoes out of the oil with a slotted spoon. Set to one side ready for the Balti.

Stage 3: Balti method
Heat the remaining oil with the onions and the cumin seeds in a large wok over a moderately high flame. Stir-fry the ginger and garlic for half a minute. Add the chilli powder and salt and stir-fry for 1 more minute. Put in the mushrooms and green peppers and stir them around in the ginger and garlic mixture for 2 minutes. Now pour in the Balti sauce and stir. Add the potatoes, garam masala and chopped coriander. Turn the heat to low and simmer, stirring often, for 10 minutes.

Divide among 4 warmed Balti bowls and serve.

THE MINAR'S AUBERGINE AND POTATO BALTI
(Proprietors the Mohammed brothers, Chef M. Sohel)

A straightforward vegetarian Balti.

4 Stages • Mild • Suitable for a dinner party or family meal • Serves 4

2 large aubergines, cubed
450 g / 1 lb potatoes, peeled
6 tbsp vegetable oil
2 small onions, chopped
5-6 ladles of Balti sauce

2 tbsp chopped fresh coriander
3 palmfuls of dried methi, rubbed over the
    wok
2 tsp chilli powder

Stage 1: Making the Balti sauce
See page 24.

Stage 2: Par-cooking the potatoes
Cook the potatoes in boiling salted water for 15 minutes. Drain and cut into cubes.

Stage 3: Frying the aubergine
Heat 3 tablespoons of the oil in a large wok over moderate heat and fry the aubergine cubes until golden brown on all sides. Remove them and place them on kitchen paper to soak up some of the oil.

Stage 4: Balti method
Put the rest of the oil in the wok and turn the heat up to moderately high. Fry the onions until translucent. Put in all the ingredients except the potatoes. Stir-fry for 3 minutes.

Add the potatoes, stir-fry for 5 more minutes and then serve, in 4 warmed Balti bowls.

MR DAVE'S SPECIAL VEGETABLE JAL FRIZIES BALTI

(Manager Qamar Zaman, Assistant Manager 'Saj'-ad Karim, Chef Habib Hussain)

An orchestration of six vegetables, and the spring onions and green pepper that define the description 'jal frizies'. This really justifies the word 'special'! No Balti sauce is needed as the way it's cooked it makes its own.

2 Stages • Mild • A vegetarian dish for a dinner party • Serves 4

900 g / 2 lb mixed vegetables:
  potatoes, carrots, dried or canned red
  kidney beans, canned tinda, shelled
  fresh or frozen peas, sliced mushrooms,
  in any proportion you like
2 tsp salt
8 tbsp vegetable oil
2 onions, grated or really finely chopped
2-3 tsp chilli powder
2 tsp turmeric powder
2 tsp garam masala (page 25)
2 tsp paprika

1-2 tsp salt
2.5 cm / 1 inch cube fresh ginger, peeled
  and grated
10 garlic cloves, crushed
4 tomatoes, chopped
2 tsp lemon juice
2 green peppers, seeded and sliced
8 spring onions, chopped
2 small tomatoes, quartered
TO GARNISH:
chopped fresh coriander
garam masala (page 25)

Stage 1: Par-cooking the vegetables

For fresh vegetables, see page 23; cook with the salt but without spices. After draining, cut the potatoes into cubes. For pre-cooking dried kidney beans, see page 24. Drain all canned vegetables.

Stage 2: Balti method

In a very large wok heat the oil over a high flame. Fry the onions until they are turning golden brown. Stirring vigorously, add the turmeric, garam masala, paprika and salt. Moisten with the ginger, garlic and chopped tomatoes, and then put in all the par-cooked vegetables. Turn the heat to low and cook, stirring gently so you don't break up the vegetables too much. If the mixture is getting dry add a little water.

After 5 minutes add the lemon juice, green peppers and spring onions, then the tomato quarters. Stir-fry for 5 more minutes.

Lift out the tomato quarters. Divide the contents of the wok among 4 warmed Balti bowls. Top with the tomato quarters and garnish each serving with a pinch of garam masala and a pinch of chopped coriander.

PARIS'S SPINACH AND CAULIFLOWER BALTI
(Proprietor Raj Mhoom, Chef Mr Mih)

Quite a simple Balti. One of the stages is par-cooking a cauliflower for about 12 minutes. Another is making a 'tarka' (aromatised oil) – about 3 minutes work while the cauliflower is cooking. This spiced oil is terracotta coloured, which contrasts well with the green and yellow of the spinach and cauliflower. It's a Balti that's subtle and different. It uses no ginger. Ginger is often omitted from vegetable dishes.

4 Stages • Mild • Vegetarian • Serves 4

680 g / 1¹/₂ lb spinach, stalks removed, chopped
450 g / 1 lb cauliflower, broken into florets
1 tsp turmeric powder
1 tsp salt
1 tsp curry powder
7 tbsp vegetable oil

1 tsp cumin seeds
1 small onion, very finely sliced into rings
¹/₂ tsp chilli powder
3 garlic cloves, very finely chopped
1 tbsp garam masala (page 25)
2 tsp dried methi, lightly ground in a mortar
5 ladles of Balti sauce

Stage 1: Par-cooking the cauliflower and spinach

Put the cauliflower florets in a large saucepan and add enough water to cover. Over a moderate flame bring to the boil. Stir in the turmeric, salt and curry powder. Cover and simmer for 5 minutes.

Add the spinach and simmer for another 5 minutes. Remove from the heat and drain the vegetables. Squeeze the spinach in a wire strainer to remove excess water.

Stage 2: Making the Balti sauce

See page 24.

Stage 3: Making the tarka

Heat 3 tablespoons of the oil in a small frying pan and add the cumin seeds. After a few seconds add the onion rings and fry them until they are golden brown. Add the chilli powder, garlic and 2 teaspoons of the garam masala and stir-fry for another minute.

Stage 4: Balti method

In a large wok heat the remaining oil and fry the ground methi and remaining garam masala for 1 minute. Add the cauliflower florets, spinach and Balti sauce. Cook gently for 3 minutes.

Divide among 4 warmed Balti bowls and pour the tarka over each Balti. Serve immediately.

PLAZA'S TARKA DAL BALTI
(Proprietor and Chef Mr R.S. 'Ravi' Ghataera)

'Dal' means lentils and split peas and the dishes they make. I double the quantity whenever I prepare dal so that it will last for another time. It never does! People, including me, keep dipping into it! There is no chance of this Balti lasting more than the one sitting. It is delicious. Serve on its own or as an accompaniment to a meat Balti.

3 Stages • Medium • Vegetarian • Serves 4

*285 g / 10 oz dried yellow split peas, or use
   2 medium cans
1 tsp turmeric powder
3/4 tsp salt
8 tbsp vegetable oil
3 tbsp chopped spring onions
4 cm / 1 1/2 inch cube fresh ginger, peeled
   and grated*

*8 garlic cloves, crushed
2 small fresh green chillies, very finely
   chopped
4 large tomatoes, roughly chopped
4-6 ladles of Balti sauce
1 1/2 tbsp chopped fresh coriander
1/2 tsp garam masala (page 25)*

Stage 1: Pre-cooking the split peas
See page 24; use the turmeric, salt and 1 litre / 1 3/4 pints water. Or open the cans and drain well.

Stage 2: Making the Balti sauce
See page 24.

Stage 3: Balti method
Heat the oil in a large wok over moderate heat and fry the spring onions, ginger and garlic for 1 minute. Put in the split peas, chillies, tomatoes and Balti sauce. Stir-fry for 4 minutes.

Add the chopped coriander. Turn the heat to low and cook gently for 2 more minutes.

Divide among 4 warmed Balti bowls and sprinkle a pinch of garam masala on each Balti. Serve with Naan bread (page 143).

PREET PALACE'S SAG CHANA (SPINACH AND CHICK PEA)

(Proprietor Mr Mittel, Chef Mr Sajjad)

We ate this with Preet Palace's Prawn Pathia (page 119). I loved this and Diane preferred the Prawn, but we both agreed that they went very well together. The dish has a deep flavour which, to me, had a hint of chocolate to it. The dish is simple enough to prepare for an indulgent one-person supper (divide everything by four if you do) but interesting enough to take its part in a dinner party menu.

4 Stages • Vegetarian • Medium • Serves 4

400 g / 14 oz spinach, cooked, drained and chopped, or use 200 g / 7 oz frozen spinach, thawed and drained
225 g / 8 oz dried chick peas or use a 425 g / 15 oz can
2 small potatoes, about 200 g / 7 oz in all, peeled and quartered
1 tsp turmeric powder
4 tbsp vegetable ghee or oil

2 cm / 3/4 inch cube fresh ginger, peeled and grated
2 garlic cloves, crushed
2 tsp salt
3 tbsp seeded and chopped green pepper
2 1/2 tbsp Balti spice mix (page 26)
1 tbsp tomato purée
2 tomatoes, chopped
2 palmfuls of chopped fresh coriander
4-6 ladles of Balti sauce

Stage 1: Pre-cooking the chick peas
See page 24. Or open the can and drain well.

Stage 2: Making the Balti sauce
See page 24.

Stage 3: Pre-cooking the potatoes
Cook the potatoes in boiling salted water, with the turmeric, until they are nearly cooked. They should still feel a little crisp inside when skewered. Drain and set them aside.

Stage 4: Balti method
Heat the ghee or oil in a large wok over a high heat. Put in the ginger, garlic and spinach. Stir well, mashing the spinach roughly. Add the salt and green pepper.

Now add the potato pieces and, as they cook, break them up. The spice mix is stirred in next, followed by the tomato purée, chick peas, tomatoes, fresh coriander and 4 ladles of Balti sauce. Shake the wok and stir vigorously, cooking for 3–4 minutes. Add more sauce if the mixture is too dry.

Divide among 4 warmed Balti dishes and serve.

RICE AND SPICE'S BALTI VEGETABLE PASANDA

(Proprietor Mr Meenar Islam, Chef Mr Shofique Miah)

Vegetable balls in a creamy sauce. The used of canned processed peas imparts a nutty flavour with a hint of dal.

3 Stages • Mildly spiced • Ideal for any Balti occasion • Serves 4

8 potatoes, peeled and chopped quite small
1 large carrot, chopped quite small
1/4 white cabbage, shredded and chopped
142 g / 5 oz canned processed marrowfat peas
115 g / 1/4 lb French beans, sliced and chopped
3 tbsp vegetable oil, plus more for deep frying
1 onion, finely chopped
1/4 green pepper, seeded and finely diced
1 tbsp salt
1 tbsp turmeric powder

1 tbsp ground coriander
1/2 tbsp chilli powder
2 handfuls of chopped fresh coriander
40 g / 1 1/2 oz golden breadcrumbs
3 eggs, lightly beaten
FOR THE SAUCE:
800 ml / 27 fl oz single cream
2 tsp dried methi
4 tbsp sugar
8 tbsp ground almonds
2 handfuls of chopped fresh coriander
25 g / 1 oz unsalted butter
1 tbsp flaked almonds

Stage 1: Cooking the vegetables

Heat the 3 tablespoons oil in a large wok over moderate heat and fry the onion and green pepper with the salt until turning brown. Add the turmeric, ground coriander and chilli powder and stir-fry for 5 more minutes.

Put in the potatoes and carrot and stir-fry for 10 minutes. Add the cabbage, peas and beans and cook for about 20 minutes or until all the vegetables are tender.

Turn the vegetable mixture into a bowl and mash together. Allow to cool.

Stage 2: Shaping and frying the vegetable balls

When the vegetable mixture is cool enough to handle, mix in 1 handful of the chopped coriander, breadcrumbs and eggs. Mould into balls about 3 cm / 1 1/4 inches in diameter.

Heat a large pan of oil. Deep-fry the vegetable balls until they are biscuit-coloured on all sides. Drain on kitchen paper.

Stage 3: Making the sauce

Mix together the cream, keeping back 2 tablespoons for garnish, the methi, sugar, ground almonds and the remaining chopped coriander. Heat the butter in the wok and gently heat the cream mixture.

Add the vegetable balls and stir-fry until heated through.

Divide among 4 warmed Balti bowls and served garnished with a dribble of cream and the flaked almonds.

ROYAL AL-FAISAL'S RED KIDNEY BEAN (KASHMIRI VALOR) BALTI
(Proprietor Mr Muhammad Ajaib)

A delicious recipe. The first stage is to make the Balti sauce, from Royal Al-Faisal's recipe for Keema Karela. Mr Ajaib says 'the secret is in the "gravy"', so if you use any other than his Balti sauce you can't call it 'Royal Al-Faisal's Red Kidney Bean Balti'!

3 Stages • Mildly spiced • Suitable for the family • Serves 4

400 g / 14 oz dried red kidney beans, or
    use canned beans
6 tbsp vegetable oil
3 handfuls of chopped fresh coriander
about 7½ ladles of Balti sauce
1 tsp dried methi
1 tsp garlic powder

5 tomatoes, chopped
1 tsp ground cloves
½ tsp ground cumin
½ tsp ground coriander
1 long thin fresh green chilli, ground in a
    mortar or finely chopped

Stage 1: Making the Balti sauce
See page 93.

Stage 2: Pre-cooking the beans
See page 24. Or open the can of beans and drain them well!

Stage 3: Balti method
Heat the oil in a large wok over a high heat. Drop in the chopped coriander and almost immediately add 6 ladles of the Balti sauce. Stir together. Sprinkle on to this the dried methi, rubbed between your palms to grind it a little, and the garlic powder.

Add the tomatoes to the wok, stirring and breaking them with up the side of the spoon. Add another ladle of Balti sauce, stir and cook over a high heat until the aroma of the garlic wafts around the kitchen (about 3 minutes).

Add the kidney beans and stir them in. Put in a little more Balti sauce if the mixture is getting too dry. Add the ground cloves ground cumin and ground coriander. Turn the heat right down, cover with a lid and simmer gently for 20 minutes.

Add the chopped chilli (or, better still, ground-in-a-mortar chilli) to the simmering wok, and cook for a further 4 minutes. If you prefer a 'wetter' dish add more Balti sauce.

Divide among 4 warmed Balti bowls and serve.

ROYAL NAIM'S BALTI DAL, VEGETABLES, SPINACH AND CHICK PEAS

(Proprietor Mr Azim, Chef Mohammad Nazir)

One saucepan, with vegetables added to a timetable, is the basis of this Balti. Pre-cooked split peas and chick peas and Balti sauce are combined with the vegetables in the wok in a final quick process.

4 Stages • Spicy • A substantial vegetarian family meal • Serves 4

450 g / 1 lb prepared mixed vegetables:
    sliced carrots, cubed aubergine,
    cauliflower florets, sliced courgettes,
    shredded cabbage, chopped spinach,
    in any proportion you like
115 g / 4 oz dried chick peas, soaked
    overnight, or use canned
115 g / 4 oz yellow split peas, or use
    canned
5 tsp Balti spice mix (page 26)
2¹/₂ tsp turmeric powder
³/₄-1 tsp salt

FOR THE BALTI STAGE:
6 tbsp vegetable ghee or oil
2 onions, chopped
2 tomatoes, chopped
2 fresh green chillies, finely chopped
4 cm / 1¹/₂ inch cube fresh ginger, peeled
    and grated
6 large garlic cloves, crushed
1¹/₂ palmfuls of chopped fresh coriander
4-5 ladles of Balti sauce
2 tsp garam masala (page 25)
2 tsp dried methi
150 ml / ¹/₄ pint plain yoghurt

Stage 1: Par-cooking the vegetables

Bring a large pan of water to the boil with the carrots, Balti spice mix and 2 teaspoons turmeric. Add the remaining vegetables in this order and at roughly these times:
    after 5 minutes add aubergine
    after 5 more minutes add cauliflower
      and courgettes
    after 5 more minutes add cabbage
    after 5 more minutes add spinach.
Cook for 5 more minutes, then drain.

Stage 2: Pre-cooking the chick peas and split peas:

Drain the chick peas and put them in a large saucepan with 900 ml / 1¹/₂ pints of water, the remaining turmeric and the salt. Bring to the boil. Cook, covered, on low heat for 30 minutes.

Add the split peas. Bring back to the boil and simmer gently for another hour or until the peas, chick and split, are just tender. Stir occasionally to prevent sticking. Drain.

Stage 3: Making the Balti sauce

See page 24.

Stage 4: Balti method

Heat the ghee or oil in a large wok over moderately high heat and fry the onions until soft. Add the tomatoes and fry them until they are pulp, breaking them up with the spoon. Add the chillies, ginger, garlic and chopped coriander. Stir-fry for 1 minute.

Put in 4 ladles of Balti sauce (the rest is for adjusting the moisture later), the garam masala, methi and the vegetables. Stir well. Add the chick peas and split peas and stir well again. Put in the yoghurt, a tablespoon at a time. Reduce the heat and simmer, stirring, for 3-4 minutes.

Divide among 4 warmed Balti bowls and serve.

SALEEM'S KARELA BALTI
(Proprietor and Chef Mr Rafiq)

Karela is a vegetable for which there is no substitute. It is called 'bitter gourd', and this recipe removes the bitterness with the help of olive oil, which makes a rare appearance in a Baltihouse.

2 Stages • Mild • Serves 4

900 g / 2 lb fresh karela, or use canned
    karela, drained and sliced
salt
5 tbsp olive oil
3 tbsp vegetable oil (not olive oil at this
    stage)
2 onions, finely sliced

6 tomatoes, chopped
1/2-1 tsp chilli powder
2 tsp turmeric powder
1 tsp garam masala (page 25)
1/4 tsp ground black pepper
1 tbsp chopped fresh coriander

Stage 1: Preparing and frying the karela

Scrape off the knobbly surface of the karelas with a potato peeler. Most of the bitterness is in the skin so this should be done thoroughly. Cut into 2 cm / 3/4 inch slices and remove any hard seeds. Rub the slices on both sides with salt and place on a tilted plate so that the bitter juice can run off. Leave for 2 hours.

Rinse the slices thoroughly under running water and pat them dry on kitchen paper. Heat the olive oil in a frying pan and fry the slices of karela until soft and turning brown. Remove the karela from the oil and drain on a wire rack.

Stage 2: Balti method

In a large wok heat the vegetable oil over moderate heat and fry the onions until golden. Stir in the tomatoes, breaking them up with the side of the spoon. Add a little salt.

Next put in the slices of karela, the chilli powder, turmeric, garam masala, black pepper and chopped coriander. Stir gently, making sure that each piece of karela is liberally coated with the onion, tomato and spices mixture. Cook for 5 more minutes.

Divide among 4 warmed Balti bowls and serve.

SHABAB'S TROPICAL VEGETABLE BALTI

(Proprietors the Hussain family, Chef Matloob Hussain)

A delicious vegetarian Balti that is adaptable to whichever vegetables are in season. Adjust the quantities for whichever vegetables you prefer to use.

2 Stages • Subtly spiced • Serves 4

1 kg / 2^{1}/$_{4}$ lb mixed vegetables: potatoes, peeled and cut into 1 cm / ^{1}/$_{2}$ inch cubes, sliced carrots, cauliflower florets, sliced courgettes, aubergine cut into 2.5 cm / 1 inch cubes, chopped cabbage, sliced button mushrooms
250 g / 9 oz spinach, large stalks removed, chopped
1 tsp salt
3 tsp turmeric powder
10 tbsp vegetable oil

4 cm / 1^{1}/$_{2}$ inch cube fresh ginger, peeled and grated
8 garlic cloves, crushed
2 tomatoes, chopped
3 small onions, chopped
2 fresh green chillies, chopped
1^{1}/$_{2}$ tbsp paprika
1 tsp garam masala (page 25)
1 tbsp chopped fresh coriander
1^{1}/$_{2}$ tbsp dried methi

Stage 1: Par-cooking the vegetables

Use a large saucepan of water. Add ^{3}/$_{4}$ teaspoon of the salt and 2 teaspoons of the turmeric. Put in the potatoes and carrots and bring to the boil. Add in this order and at roughly these times:

after 5 minutes the cauliflower and courgettes
after 3 more minutes the aubergine and cabbage
after 3 more minutes the spinach

Remove from the heat and drain, keeping back a cup of the water. Keep the vegetables warm.

Stage 2: Balti method

Heat the oil in a large wok over moderate heat and fry the ginger and garlic for 1 minute. Put in the tomatoes and the onions. Add the rest of the salt and the chillies. Cook, stirring, until the onions are soft. Add the rest of the turmeric and the paprika. Stir-fry for 5 minutes.

Put in the mushrooms and par-cooked vegetables and add a little of the vegetables' water if the mixture seems too dry. Continue to cook, stirring all the time and occasionally testing by taste to check when the vegetables are heated through. When they are, add the garam masala, chopped coriander and methi. Stir-fry for a couple of minutes more. Adjust the seasoning.

Remove from the heat. If there is too much oil spoon it off. Divide among 4 warmed Balti bowls and serve.

SHER KHAN'S SHABJI (VEGETABLE) BALTI
(Chef Mr Saeed)

An argument for vegetarian food as far as we are concerned! Broccoli and courgettes make rare appearances in this Balti.

4 Stages • Mildly spiced • For a vegetarian dinner party • Serves 4

115 g / 1/4 lb potatoes, peeled (and diced roughly after cooking)
85 g / 3 oz carrots, sliced
85 g / 3 oz broccoli florets
145 g / 5 oz courgettes, thickly sliced
225 g / 1/2 lb aubergine, diced
1 large red pepper, seeded and diced
85 g / 3 oz ladies' fingers (okra)
250 g / 9 oz fresh spinach, chopped
2 ladles of pre-cooked chick peas, or use canned

2 ladles of pre-cooked yellow split peas
FOR THE BALTI STAGE:
6 tbsp vegetable oil
2.5 cm / 1 inch cube fresh ginger, peeled and grated
3 large garlic cloves, crushed
4 ladles of Balti sauce
1 small tomato, chopped
1/4 tsp chilli powder
a small palmful of dried methi
garam masala to garnish (page 25)

Stage 1: Making the Balti sauce
See page 24.

Stage 2: Pre-cooking the chick peas and split peas
See page 24.

Stage 3: Par-cooking the vegetables
Put a large saucepan with plenty of salted water on the stove. Add the potatoes and carrots and bring to the boil. Add the other vegetables in this order and at roughly these times (keep testing: the vegetables should not be overcooked):

after 5 minutes the broccoli and courgettes

after 3 more minutes the aubergine and red pepper

after 3 more minutes the ladies' fingers and spinach

When all the vegetables are tender, with a little of their natural crunch still left, remove from the heat and drain. Dice the potatoes. Keep the vegetables warm for the Balti stage.

Stage 4: Balti method
Heat the oil in a large wok over moderate heat and fry the ginger and garlic. After 1 minute stir in the Balti sauce and tomato. Stir-fry until the tomato is pulped. Add the chilli powder, methi, chick peas and the par-cooked vegetables. Stir them well, then put in the split peas. Stir-fry for 3 minutes.

Divide among 4 warmed Balti bowls and garnish each with a sprinkle of garam masala.

BREADS, SWEETS AND ACCOMPANIMENTS

BALTI NAANS

There are lots of choices in supermarkets nowadays, including stuffed naans, but this recipe is as simple as making ordinary bread and is well worth the effort, if only to boast that you can stand alongside any Balti Tandoori Chef with pride.

Makes 4

2 tsp sugar
1 tsp dried yeast
1/2 cup warm water
4 tbsp milk
1 1/2 tsp baking powder
2 tbsp vegetable oil

1/4 tsp bicarbonate of soda
1 egg
225 g / 8 oz plain flour
1/4 tsp salt
melted butter

Dissolve 1/2 teaspoon of the sugar and the yeast in the warm water. Set aside in a warm place until frothy.

Warm the milk in a small saucepan. Take it off the heat and add the baking powder, oil, bicarbonate of soda and egg. Whisk together.

Sift the flour and salt into a mixing bowl and add the rest of the sugar. Make a depression in the middle and pour in the warmed milk and egg mixture. Add the yeast mixture. Mix to make a dough.

Turn the dough on to a floured surface and knead for 10 minutes or until smooth and elastic. Return to the bowl, cover with a damp tea towel and leave to rise in a warm place until the dough has risen to 1 1/2 times its original volume. This will take about 1 hour. Divide into 4 equal balls, sprinkling your hands with more flour. Cover and leave again in a warm place to rise for 15 minutes.

Preheat the grill. Keeping the other 3 balls covered, take one of the balls and flatten and roll it into a pear-shape about 25 cm / 10 inches long. Put your tava or a heavy-based frying pan on a moderately high heat. When the tava is hot moisten one side of the naan with water and slap it on the tava. Cook until it puffs up, then quickly transfer it to the hot grill to brown the top slightly. Brush with melted butter and seal in foil to keep hot. Repeat the process to make 3 more naan.

You can also bake the naans on a heavy baking tray in a very hot oven. Finish off the tops under the grill.

BALTI GARLIC NAANS

Add 8 cloves of garlic, roughly chopped, to the dough after it has been rising for 1 hour and before you divide it into 4.

CHAPATIS

Chapatis are very easy to make once you've got the knack. They're best eaten with generous-portioned Baltis or those with a rich sauce (naan bread is bulkier and more filling). Chapatis have the advantage health-wise because they're made with whole-wheat flour. They freeze very well.

Makes approximately 15

255 g / 8 oz whole-wheat flour
1 tsp salt
170 ml / 6 fl oz water

Mix the flour and salt together in a bowl. Gradually add the water, mixing with a spoon and then your fingers, to make a dough. Knead the dough for about 5 minutes or until it is supple and elastic. Cover with a damp cloth and leave to stand for 30 minutes.

Dust flour on to a work surface. Divide the dough into 15 small balls, each roughly the size of a walnut. Taking one ball at a time, press it lightly on to the floured surface and roll out into a disc about 14 cm / 5¹/₂ inches in diameter, dusting frequently with flour. The chapatis should be as thin as parchment paper.

Heat a tava or heavy-based frying pan and cook each chapati on a low heat for 30 seconds on each side. Look for a bubbly effect on the surface. Set the tava or pan aside.

Now for the good bit. Turn your gas flame to high or your electric element to the highest setting. Using a fish slice hold the chapatis, one at a time, over the heat for a few seconds. They'll puff up immediately.

To serve, stack the chapatis in a warmed deep dish lined with a napkin. Alternatively, you could seal the stack of chapatis in foil until your Baltis are ready and then reheat in the oven at 220°C / 425°F / gas mark 7 for 15-20 minutes. They can also be reheated quickly in the microwave (without the foil wrapping).

AHMED'S BALTI DIP
(Proprietor and Chef Mr Ahmed)

A slightly different, subtly spiced and sweetish dip.

Serves 6

200 ml / 7 fl oz plain yoghurt
1 tsp concentrated mint sauce
1 tsp sugar
1 tsp lime pickle
1 tsp mango pickle

1 tsp chilli pickle, or use ¹/₂ fresh green
  chilli, finely chopped
1 tsp sweet mango chutney
1 tbsp chopped fresh coriander
yellow food colouring (optional)

Put all the ingredients into a blender or food processor and liquidise.

Serve with Chicklamas, pakoras or poppadoms.

SPICE VALLEY'S BALTI DIP

Serves 6

200 ml / 7 fl oz plain yoghurt
1 heaped tsp mango pickle
1 heaped tsp mango chutney
¹/₂ tsp lemon juice
1 tsp chopped fresh coriander

¹/₄ fresh green chilli, chopped
1 heaped tsp concentrated mint sauce
1 heaped tsp sugar
pinch of salt
pinch of chilli powder

Put all the ingredients except the yoghurt in a blender or food processor and liquidise until smooth. Add the yoghurt and blend to a smooth pale green dip with speckles of dark green.

Serve with warmed plain poppadoms.
Note: For extra kick, substitute lime pickle and lime chutney for mango. Add an extra teaspoon of sugar to offset the bite of the lime.

MOKHAM'S IMLI (TAMARIND) SAUCE

(Proprietors 'Naz' and 'Kal', Chef 'Kal')

Tamarind is an exotic, bitter fruit which has a taste all its own. You can find dried tamarind compressed into blocks in Asian shops. This has to be soaked overnight, but the actual sauce takes just minutes and makes a marvellous sweet and sour dip to eat with poppadoms, or a sauce to go with spicy lamb starters or pakoras.

Serves 4-6

200 g / 7 oz block of compressed tamarind
1 small onion, roughly chopped
1/2 green pepper, seeded and roughly
    chopped
1 heaped tsp chopped fresh coriander
1/2 tsp salt

1 tbsp sugar
1 tsp concentrated mint sauce
1 1/2 heaped tbsp tomato ketchup
a few drops of red food colouring
    (optional)

Put the tamarind in a bowl with 300 ml / 1/2 pint of water and leave to soak overnight. Make sure all the tamarind is broken up into the water so the juice will be extracted. Squeeze the pulp and strain the liquid into another bowl.

Put the chopped onion, green pepper and coriander in a blender and blend to a paste. Add the rest of the ingredients and the strained tamarind liquid and blend until smooth.

JOHN BACON'S SPECIAL BALTI LIME PICKLE

Lime pickle is used in a number of Balti dips and a few recipes. There are several brands on the market, but nothing beats making your own. This recipe makes a potent pickle that looks highly decorative on the shelf. It's edible in 2 months, but really gets into its stride in about a year. Mature it in bright sunlight.

Makes a 1.5 litre / 2¹/₂ pint jar quantity

*15 fresh limes, halved, each half cut into
    3 pieces, and pipped*
500 ml / 18 fl oz distilled malt vinegar
115 g / 4 oz caster sugar
*1 lemon, cut 3 slices and cut the peel of the
    rest into very fine strips (optional)*
8 garlic cloves, each cut into 3 pieces
*4 cm / 1¹/₂ inch cube fresh ginger, peeled
    and cut into chunks a litle larger than*

the garlic pieces
*12 fresh green chillies, finely sliced
    lengthways*
25 g / 1 oz black mustard seeds
25 g / 1 oz yellow mustard seeds
4 tbsp grated fresh ginger
110 g / 3³/₄ oz sea salt
*3-4 dried kaffir lime leaves
    (optional)*

Put the vinegar and sugar in a large saucepan and bring to the boil. Boil gently until the mixture starts to thicken. Set aside to cool.

Meanwhile, sterilise the jar, but don't dry the inside.

The pickle is made up in layers. If you are using the lemon, put the 3 slices on the bottom of the jar. Put a layer of lime pieces in the jar. Add a few pieces of garlic, then ginger, a layer of chilli, a layer of mustard seeds, ¹/₂ teaspoon of ginger, a few strips of lemon peel and a scant tablespoon of sea salt. Repeat the layering until the jar is full. If you are using the lime leaves, break them up and tuck in every two or three layers. They will give a slight background bite.

Pour in the cooled vinegar syrup and seal the jar.

LASSI

Yoghurt has always been the traditional cooling agent to spicy food. Sipped as a drink it's much more effective than a pint of lager for putting out the fire. Drinking yoghurt is known as 'lassi' and you can drink it sweet, salted or flavoured.

SALTED LASSI

Serves 4-6

300 ml / ½ pint plain yoghurt
1 tsp salt

freshly ground black pepper
crushed ice or ice cubes

Liquidise the yoghurt and 1.2 litres / 2 pints water together in a blender until nice and frothy. Stir in the salt and some freshly ground pepper to taste. Pour into a jug, add the ice and serve in tall glasses.

Note: At the blending stage you can add 1 teaspoon of chopped fresh mint, fresh coriander or fresh methi.

SWEET LASSI

Serves 4-6

300 ml / ½ pint plain yoghurt
2-3 tsp caster sugar

a few drops of kewra essence
crushed ice or ice cubes

Put all the ingredients (except the ice) into a blender and add 900 ml / 1½ pints of water. Liquidise until frothy. Add the crushed ice and serve in tall glasses. A delicious drink for a hot day. You don't even need the excuse of a Balti.

THICK MANGO MILK SHAKE

For children, and for adults who still think they are kids. This is a drink with a distinct tang of another continent and with all the goodness of fresh fruit.

Makes about 1.2 litres / 2 pints

2 large fresh mangoes, peeled and stoned,
* or use 2 x 425 g / 15 oz cans sliced*
* mangoes, drained*
600 ml / 1 pint milk

4 tbsp caster sugar
1 tsp ground very lightly roasted green
* cardamom seeds*

Prepare a couple of hours before serving.

If you're using fresh mangoes, slice the flesh into 2.5 cm / 1 inch pieces. Put the mangoes, half the milk, the sugar and cardamom into a blender or food processor and liquidise until thick and creamy.

Pour into a large jug. Add 300 ml / 1/2 pint of water and the rest of the milk and stir. Cover and chill for a couple of hours.

Serve the milk shake in tall glasses with plenty of crushed ice.

JEERA (CUMIN SEED) CRUSH

A light, delicately spiced appetiser that's renowned in Balti circles as an aid to digestion. Sipped during the meal, it takes the heat out of the hottest Balti.

Serves 4

2 tbsp cumin seeds
2 dried red chillies, crushed
15 g / 1/2 oz fresh mint leaves, chopped

1 tsp salt
1 tsp sugar
1 tbsp lemon juice

Prepare at least 2 hours ahead to allow for chilling before you serve it.

Dry-roast the cumin seeds in a cast-iron tava or heavy-based frying pan until they change colour. Crush them lightly in a mortar.

Bring 600 ml / 1 pint of water to the boil in a saucepan. Add the cumin and the rest of the ingredients except the lemon juice. Cover the pan and simmer for 15 minutes.

Remove from the heat and stir in the lemon juice. Strain, allow to cool and then chill.

DIANE AND MIKE'S PISTACHIO KULFI (ICE CREAM)

(Chefs Diane Lowe and Mike Davidson)

This involves up to 1¹/₂ hours of watching and stirring milk while it slowly boils and reduces. Bring a chair and a crossword puzzle to the stove! It is well worth the effort.

Makes about 450 ml/³/₄ pint

1.2 litres / 2 pints milk
6 green cardamoms, broken slightly open
2 tbsp sugar

15 g / ¹/₂ oz ground almonds
25 g / 1 oz shelled and skinned unsalted pistachio nuts, ground

Bring the milk to the boil in a heavy-based saucepan. Simmer as fast as you dare, stirring often, turning the skin in as it forms.

After 30 minutes add the cardamoms. Continue boiling the milk until it is reduced to about 450 ml / ³/₄ pint. It will be a wonderful pinky-yellow colour! Remove the cardamom pods.

Add the sugar, almonds and pistachios. Stir and cook gently for 3 more minutes. Remove from the heat, pour into a bowl and allow to cool completely.

Cover the bowl with cling film and place in the freezer. After 30 minutes remove and give the mixture a good stir to prevent ice crystals forming. Replace in the freezer. Remove again and stir at 20 minute intervals, replacing each time in the freezer.

Meanwhile, put enough ice lolly moulds for this quantity into the freezer to chill. Alternatively use washed individual yoghurt pots, although these do make rather large portions.

When the ice cream becomes difficult to stir spoon it quickly into the lolly moulds or yoghurt pots. Seal them with foil and freeze solid.

To serve dip the moulds or pots in warm water to loosen the ice cream. Invert on to small chilled plates.

CHERRY BARFI

Barfi is a sort of Asian fudge. It's a great favourite in 'Sweet Centres' and makes a good pud to follow a Balti.

Serves 6-8

600 ml / 1 pint milk
a few green cardamoms
225 g / 8 oz ground almonds

285 g / 10 oz caster sugar
285 g / 10 oz unsalted butter or ghee
25 g / 1 oz glacé cherries, halved

Put the milk in a saucepan and drop in the cardamoms. Heat gently to release the spice flavour into the milk, then discard them.

Put the ground almonds into a blender and gradually add the flavoured milk to make a stiff paste.

Heat the sugar and 3 tablespoons water in a heavy-based saucepan over low heat, stirring into a thick syrup. Add the almond paste and stir together until evenly mixed.

In another saucepan melt the butter or

ghee. When the almond paste mixture starts to boil add the melted fat a little at a time, waiting for the fat to separate and rise to the surface each time before adding any more. When all the fat is incorporated add the glacé cherries. Remove from the heat and allow to cool for a few minutes.

Spread the mixture in a lightly greased shallow rectangular dish to make a 2.5 cm / 1 inch thickness. Leave in a cool place until set. Cut into roughly 2.5 cm / 1 inch squares for serving.

ALMOND HALVA

Home-made halva is very popular in the Balti Belt's 'Sweet Centres'. Just like in every other pâtisserie you pick your 'sweets' – halva and barfi – have them boxed and wrapped and enjoy them as a weekend treat. This halva takes about 15 minutes to make.

Serves 6-8

115 g / 4 oz unsalted butter
115 g / 4 oz ground semolina
115 g / 4 oz ground almonds
115 g / 4 oz caster sugar

1/2 tsp ground nutmeg
300 ml / 1/2 pint milk
25 g / 1 oz toasted flaked almonds

Melt the butter in a heavy-based saucepan over a low heat. Put in the semolina and cook until golden, stirring to prevent lumps and burning. Add the ground almonds, sugar and nutmeg and stir them in thoroughly. Add the milk, a little at a time, stirring until the mixture thickens.

Pour into a small greased rectangular dish, no less than 2.5 cm / 1 inch deep. Spread the mixture evenly to 1-2 cm / 1/2 - 3/4 inch thickness. Sprinkle almond flakes on top and press them gently in. Allow to cool.

Cut into 2.5 cm / 1 inch squares for serving.

FIRNI

Not a 'Sweet Centre' pastry but an aromatic rice-based pudding that has a plush, exotic taste and texture. Good for cooling down after a Balti blow-out.

Serves 4-6

300 ml / $\frac{1}{2}$ pint milk
40 g / 1$\frac{1}{2}$ oz ground rice
1 tbsp ground almonds
400 g /14 oz can of evaporated milk
55 g / 2 oz caster sugar
1 tbsp rosewater
1 tsp ground cardamom

25 g / 1 oz flaked almonds
25 g / 1 oz shelled unsalted pistachio nuts, lightly crushed
15 g / $\frac{1}{2}$ oz unsalted cashew nuts, roughly chopped
25 g / 1 oz dried apricot, finely chopped

Bring the milk to the boil, adding the ground rice and ground almonds as the milk is heating. Stirring constantly, add the evaporated milk and sugar. Cook over a low heat for about 5 minutes. Remove the pan from the heat and allow to cool, stirring from time to time to prevent skin forming on top.

Add the rosewater and cardamom and most of the flaked almonds, pistachios, cashews and apricot to the mixture. Transfer to a glass bowl and decorate with the remaining nuts and fruit.

Serve hot or cold.

GLOSSARY

Acharie Pickle

Ajwan Lovage seeds

Aloo Potato

Amchur Mango powder

Atta Wholemeal flour used for chapatis

Barfi Sweet. Cross between marzipan and fudge

Battera Quail

Bhindi Ladies' fingers or okra

Bhuna A dryish dish with little sauce

Cardamom Pods, either brown or green

Chana Chick peas

Cholley Chick peas

Coriander The leaves are used fresh, the seeds are used whole or ground

Cumin Seeds with a hint of caraway taste. White ones are more common and readily available, especially ground. Black are used in some garam masalas and bouquet garnis

Dal Lentils. Yellow split peas are most common in these recipes

Dhania Coriander, both herb and seed

Dhansak Sweet and sour, with lentils

Dopiaza 'Two onions'. Some are fried and added later

Fenugreek Used in these recipes exclusively in leaf form, fresh or, more often, dried

Galangal Related to ginger and can be used as a substitute. Sometimes available fresh, but usually dried or powdered, from Asian or Chinese shops

Garam masala An aromatic spice mixture, available ready-made but much better freshly ground and mixed

Ghee Clarified butter or vegetable fat

Ghobi Cauliflower

Gosht Lamb, or meat in general

Gram flour Ground chick peas

Haldi Turmeric

Imli Tamarind

Jalfrezi Dish cooked with spring onions and green peppers

Jeera (Zeera) Cumin

Kalonji Onion seeds

Karahi (Korai) A Balti dish or wok

Karela Bitter gourd

Keema Minced meat

Kewra A flavouring essence used in sweets

Kofta Meat or vegetable ball

Koorma Dish cooked with nuts and cream

Kulfi Ice cream

Lassi Yoghurt-based drink

Makhani Dish cooked with nuts, milk, cream and yoghurt

Masala mixture

Methi Fenugreek

Moghlai Cooked in the style of the Moghuls

Murghi Chicken

Naan Leavened puffy flat bread

Pakora Fritter

Palak Spinach

Paneer Compressed cottage cheese

Pasanda With a sweetish sauce of cream and almonds

Pathia Hot, sweet and sour

Puri Deep-fried chapati

Rogan Josh A paprika-red dish

Sag Spinach

Shabji Vegetables

S(h)eek Skewer

Tarka Spiced oil

Tava Single handled, slightly concave griddle for cooking naan and chapatis on top of the stove

Tikka Skewered. Now often means 'off-the-bone'

Tikki Round fritter

ACKNOWLEDGEMENTS AND MAIL ORDER

Our grateful thanks to Maggie and Arthur for providing a base in Edgbaston. To John Bacon who trawled the wine racks of Britain with such hedonistic enthusiasm, and to all the Baltihouse managers and chefs who contributed so much to this book. Our thanks, too, to Andy Munro whose in-depth knowledge of Baltihouses was invaluable.

Where to find the Baltihouses featured in this book:

Adil 130 & 148 Stoney Lane, Sparkbrook, Birmingham B12 8AQ

Ahmed 4 High Street, Lye, Stourbridge, West Midlands DY9 8JT

Akash 1425 Pershore Road, Stirchley, Birmingham B30 2JL

Alamgeer 811 Stratford Road, Sparkhill, Birmingham B11 4DA

Al Moughal 622 Bearwood Road, Edgbaston, Birmingham B66 4BW

Balti Bazaar 1267-1269 Pershore Road, Stirchley, Birmingham B30 2YT

Balti Society 64 New Street, Birmingham B2 4DU

Balti Towers 85 Long Lane, Halesowen, West Midlands B62 9DJ

Bhangra Beat 17-21 Sternhold Avenue, Streatham Hill, London SW2 4DA

Brick Lane's Sonar Bangla 46 Hanbury Street, London E1

Butts (re-named Tabaq) 373 Stratford Road, Sparkhill, Birmingham B11 4AB

Celebrity Balti 44 Broad Street, Birmingham B1 2EW

Channi's 795 Stratford Road, Sparkhill, Birmingham B11 1AG

Diwan 3b Alcester Road, Moseley, Birmingham B13 8AR

Empire 162 Stratford Road, Sparkbrook, Birmingham B11

Faisal Sundown 639 Washwood Heath Road, Ward End, Birmingham B8 2HJ

Grand Tandoori 343-345 Stratford Road, Sparkhill, Birmingham B11 4JY

High Quality 66-68 & 97 Lozells Road, Birmingham B12 2TP

I am King (of Balti) 230-232 Ladypool Road, Sparkbrook, Birmingham B12 8JT

Ib-ne-Ghani 266 Green Lane, Small Heath, Birmingham B9 5DL

Imran 264-266 Ladypool Road, Sparkbrook, Birmingham B12 8JU

Istafa 6 Hales Street, Coventry, West Midlands CV1 1JD

Kababish 29 Woodbridge Road, Moseley, Birmingham B13 8EH

Kababish 266 Jockey Road, Sutton Coldfield, West Midlands B73 5XP

Kababish 2 Robin Hood Island, Hall Green, Birmingham B28 0LN

Kamran 34 High Street, Lye, Stourbridge, West Midlands DY9 8ST

Khan 632 Bristol Road, Selly Oak, Birmingham B29 6BQ

Khanum 510 Bristol Road, Selly Oak, Birmingham B29 6BQ

Khyber 365 Ladypool Road, Sparkbrook, Birmingham B12 8LA

Khyber Pass 104 Alum Rock Road, Saltley, Birmingham B8

Kirran 483 Coventry Road, Small Heath, Birmingham B10 0JS

Memsahib 363 High Street, West Bromwich, West Midlands

Minar 7 Walford Road, Sparkbrook, Birmingham B11 1AG

Mokham's 140 Digbeth, Birmingham B5 6DR

Mr Dave's High Street, Lye, Stourbridge, West Midlands DY9 8ST

Nirala 530 Moseley Road, Moseley, Birmingham B12 9AE

Paris 48a Alum Rock Road, Saltley, Birmingham B8 1JA

Panjab Tandoori (departed and mourned by us!)

Plaza 278-280 Ladypool Road, Sparkbrook, Birmingham B12 8JU

Preet Palace 127 Ladypool Road, Sparkbrook, Birmingham B12 8JU

Punjab Paradise 377 Ladypool Road, Sparkbrook, Birmingham B12 8JU

Raja 432 Bearwood Road, Bearwood, Birmingham B66 4EY

Rice and Spice 160 Stoke Newington High Street, London N16 0JL

Royal Al-Faisal 136-140 Stoney Lane, Sparkbrook, Birmingham 8AQ

Royal Naim 417-419 Stratford Road, Sparkhill, Birmingham B11 4JZ

Royal Watan 602-604 Pershore Road, Selly Park, Birmingham B30 2JL

Ruby's 260-262 Stratford Road, Shirley, Solihull, West Midlands B90 3AG

Saleem 256-258 Ladypool Road, Sparkbrook, Birmingham B12 8JU

Salma 667 Stratford Road, Sparkhill, Birmingham B11 4DY

Shabab 163-165 Ladypool Road, Sparkbrook, Birmingham B12 8JY

Shahenshah 326-328 Ladypool Road, Sparkbrook, Birmingham B12 8JY

Sheereen Kadah 543 Moseley Road, Balsall Heath, Birmingham B12 9AN

Sher Khan 358-360 Stratford Road, Sparkhill, Birmingham B11 4AB

Spice Valley 706 Stratford Road, Sparkhill, Birmingham B11 4DA

Yasser 1268 Pershore Road, Stirchley, Birmingham B30 2XU

MAIL ORDER DETAILS

For full details and a price list of our mail order service, which includes Balti bowls, tavas and Balti spices, send a stamped addressed envelope to:

The Baltihouse Kitchen, PO Box 4401, Henley-on-Thames, OXON.RG9 1FW

INDEX